Conditional Citizens

Conditional Citizens

On Belonging in America

Laila Lalami

Pantheon Books, New York

Small portions of this book appeared, in different form, in
The Nation, The Los Angeles Times, The New Yorker online,
and *The New York Times Magazine.*

Library of Congress Cataloging-in-Publication Data
Names: Lalami, Laila, [date] author.
Title: Conditional citizens: on belonging in America /
Laila Lalami.
Description: First Edition. New York: Pantheon Books, 2020.
Includes bibliographical references.
Identifiers: LCCN 2019037549 (print).
LCCN 2019037550 (ebook). ISBN 9781524747169 (hardcover).
ISBN 9781524747176 (ebook).
Subjects: LCSH: Citizenship—United States. United States—
Emigration and immigration. Naturalization—United States.
Discrimination—United States.
Classification: LCC JK1759.L223 2020 (print) |
LCC JK1759 (ebook) | DDC 323.60973—dc23
LC record available at lccn.loc.gov/2019037549
LC ebook record available at lccn.loc.gov/2019037550

www.pantheonbooks.com

Jacket image: (U.S.A. passport seal) Alamy
Jacket design by Linda Huang

Printed in the United States of America
First Edition
2 4 6 8 9 7 5 3 1

For Alex

CONTENTS

Conditional Citizens

—

Allegiance

This is a story about love and country, and I will tell it to you how I remember it, in strands that took me years to untangle and then thread together. I became an American on a sweltering day in 2000, a day when the marine layer over Los Angeles cleared off before breakfast. The exact date had been circled on my wall calendar with the same blue Sharpie I used to mark holidays, and I thought of it as an equally festive occasion, the culmination of a journey that had begun when I came to the United States as a foreign student eight years earlier. Over the course of those years, I had adopted, almost without realizing it, two of the more emblematic trappings of that particular era: I worked for a technology startup company and drove an SUV for which I had no discernible need. The deregulation of banks, the war in the Balkans, and Bill Clinton's angry denials that he did not have sex with that woman were in the past. The NASDAQ was at a record high; unemployment was at a record low. The future seemed full of possibility.

The citizenship ceremony was held at the Pomona Fairplex, a 487-acre facility best known for hosting the Los Angeles County Fair every summer. I remember wearing a sleeveless dress, a silver necklace my mother had given me, and a pair of new shoes that blistered my feet. My husband was in the same black suit and tie he had worn at our wedding. Ushers directed us to Building Four, a large, gray hall where I turned in my alien-registration card and was handed a miniature flag in return. Folding chairs had been set up in two columns: those who were to be sworn in had to sit on the left side of the aisle, their guests on the right.

At precisely 9:00 a.m., the first few notes of "The Star-Spangled Banner" played on the loudspeaker, and a hush fell over the audience. The air smelled of fresh roses and heavy cologne, but the mix could not fully disguise the scent of three thousand people gathered in a windowless hall in ninety-eight-degree weather. The presiding judge, an elderly man in wire-rimmed glasses, came to the lectern and delivered a homily about the rights and responsibilities that awaited us. Citizenship was a privilege we had earned, he said, and we were to honor it by participating in civic life—voting in elections, serving on juries, even running for office. He had kindly eyes and a warm demeanor; it seemed impossible that he would ever pass a cruel or unfair sentence on anyone in his courtroom. After his speech, he moved to the center of the stage and asked us to stand so that we could recite the oath of allegiance. I raised my right hand.

Love had brought me to that moment. When I came to the United States, my intention had been to complete a doctoral degree in linguistics and return home to Morocco, where I hoped to work as a college professor. But one day I met a man who made me reconsider many things, not least of which my distrust of romance. Alex and I had nothing in common—he was a network engineer, listened to grunge music, liked to spend entire weekends hiking up one mountain or another in Southern California. My hobbies were limited to reading. Still, whenever we were together, we lost track of time. I remember us driving to a movie in Century City one night, and missing the freeway exit twice because we were so engrossed in our conversation. After it became clear that our relationship was serious, we realized that one of us had to live in the other's country. I was young and in love; I made a commitment to my husband and another to his homeland.

I applied for permanent residency, a process that required submitting to a background check, sending in tax returns, going on interviews, and jumping through various bureaucratic hoops. One day, a notice arrived from the Department of Justice informing me that I was eligible for naturalization. I spent weeks studying for the citizenship exam. Alex helped by quizzing me while we were eating dinner or washing dishes. How many voting members are there in the House of Representatives? Four hundred and thirty-five. Who wrote the Declaration of Independence? Thomas Jefferson. What stops a branch of government from being too powerful? Checks and balances. But in the end, I didn't find the test particularly challenging. Perhaps it was because, long before setting foot in the United States, I had taken courses on its history, studied its literature, and become fluent in its culture. (The familiarity, I realized within days of arriving in California, was not mutual.)

Then the moment came when I had to take the oath. I swore to renounce allegiance and fidelity to any foreign prince of whom I had been a subject, to support and defend the Constitution and laws of the United States, and to bear true faith to the same. Faith was an apt word for the leap I was taking: I was placing my trust in America. Alex and I came out of Building Four, holding hands and squinting in the sunlight. Later that morning, he dropped me off at my office, and an hour later I was called to a meeting. I opened the door to the conference room to find my colleagues—lexicographers and programmers and business analysts—huddled together under red, white, and blue balloons. "Surprise!" they hollered in unison. On the table was a catered lunch of hamburgers, apple pie, and lemonade.

As I said, a festive occasion.

Nearly twenty years have passed since that summer morning at the Pomona Fairplex. I am no longer a starry-eyed bride, but maturity has its advantages: I can see better now what I had perceived only dimly back then. Being a citizen of the United States, I had thought, meant being an equal member of the American family—a spirited group of people of different races, origins, and creeds, bound together by common ideals. As time went by, however, the contradictions between doctrine and reality became harder to ignore. While my life in this country is in most ways happy and fulfilling, it has never been entirely secure or comfortable. Certain facts regularly stand in the way, facts that make of me a conditional citizen. By this I mean that my relationship to the state, observed through exposure to its policies or encounters with its representatives, is affected in all sorts of ways by my being an immigrant, a woman, an Arab, and a Muslim.

Shortly after taking the oath, I applied for and received an American passport. The blue booklet was at once a tangible proof of my new citizenship and a powerful artifact that gave me the freedom to travel without restriction to more than 150 countries. I made immediate use of it when I flew to Hong Kong in October 2000 to attend the annual meeting of the Association for Computational Linguistics. Alex had decided to tag along, and we spent a few days sightseeing on the island and in the Kowloon peninsula. Coming back to the U.S., we went through Customs at Los Angeles International Airport, both of us relieved not to have to go in separate lines anymore. When we walked up to the counter, the border agent examined both of our passports, then turned to my husband. "So," he said, his face breaking into a conspiratorial smile, "how many camels did you have to trade in for her?"

This was my first interaction with an agent of the state since I'd become a citizen, and the direction it took so stunned me that I was rendered speechless. I think I might have gasped, because the agent threw back his head and laughed, his face as pink as a new scar. With a wink at Alex, he stamped my passport and waved us both through. I was furious, and when I told a friend about it later, she said to forget it, it was just a stupid joke. "Don't read too much into it," she said. But I am a writer, and what is a writer if not someone who reads into things? Ten years later, the experience happened again, in almost identical detail, at John F. Kennedy Airport. We were returning from a vacation in Morocco and this time, my husband was asked whether he'd had to trade some cows for me.

Twice, I had come face-to-face with the state, in the person of the border agent, and discovered that it held a specific bias about me as a citizen. The two encounters reflect an enduring perception in the United States—by no means restricted to border agents—of Arabs and Muslims as lesser people: their religions, languages, cultures, customs, and modes of dress are marked not only as different but also inferior. The perception flows from representations in popular media, whose purpose is less to illuminate or engage Arab Muslim life than it is to assert its deficiency and justify its subjugation, a dynamic that Edward Said described forty years ago in *Orientalism*. In a comprehensive survey of representation in Hollywood films, for example, the critic Jack Shaheen found that more than 90 percent of movies that featured Arab Muslim characters portrayed them negatively. These images are ubiquitous and influential—so influential that they can make otherwise sensible people believe that they are true. The complexity of a multitude of private experiences is erased and replaced by a single public story, which grows more convincing with each repetition.

When a community struggles against such erasure, I would soon learn, even a small glance of acknowledgment from a politician can feel like an immense validation. A couple of months after I took the oath, Alex and I went to a mosque on Vermont Avenue to donate blood for a drive organized by the American Red Cross. While I stood on the sidewalk, waiting my turn to have my blood drawn, I was handed a flyer from the Muslim Public Affairs Council asking me to vote for George W. Bush in the upcoming election. I can't recall the specific wording of it, but the basic argument was that Ralph Nader was unelectable, Al Gore didn't espouse family values, but George Bush cared about issues that mattered to the community. When Alex came out of the Red Cross truck, I showed him the flyer. "Why him?" I wondered out loud. "I don't understand." Only later did it occur to me that Bush had made these people—my people—feel like they were seen and heard for the first time.

As presidential candidate, Bush had courted the Arab and Muslim vote. He traveled to Dearborn, Michigan, which has a large Arab-American population, to meet with community leaders, and appointed an Arab-American lobbyist, Khaled Saffuri, as an adviser to his campaign. During one of his televised debates with Al Gore, Bush pledged to end racial profiling in encounters with law enforcement and to stop the use of secret evidence in immigration proceedings, both sensitive issues within the Arab and Muslim communities. At the First Union Center in Philadelphia, where the Republican National Convention was held that year, Bush invited Talat Othman, a

Palestinian-American businessman, to deliver a Muslim benediction. This marked the first time that an Islamic prayer had been included in a major party's convention, a novelty that pundits highlighted during television coverage of the events.

Bush's strategy ultimately paid off. He received more than 45,000 votes from various Muslim communities in Florida, a state he carried, thanks to the Supreme Court's interference in the recount, by just 537 votes. Notably, however, black Muslims remained unconvinced by Bush's claims that he was "a different kind of Republican"—a conservative who would rally "little armies of compassion" to address persistent social problems like drug abuse or teen pregnancy—and by wide margins chose Al Gore instead. The "Muslim vote" was not monolithic, it turned out. Black Muslims had a different perception of Bush than non-black Muslims, many of whom seemed either unaware or unconcerned about the racist flyers that were sent in support of his candidacy during the race for the Republican nomination in South Carolina. Openly pursued for the first time by a presidential candidate, and apparently persuaded by his campaign promises, Arab Muslims cast their ballots for him.

The day after Bush was sworn into office, a group of prominent Republicans, including Newt Gingrich and Grover Norquist, met with representatives from the Arab and Muslim communities to discuss issues of concern, including racial profiling. Legislation to stop the practice was introduced in Congress—by Russ Feingold, a Democrat. To remind Bush of his campaign commitments to them, Arab and Muslim leaders asked to meet with him directly. The appointment, much discussed and much delayed, was finally scheduled for 3:30 p.m. on Tuesday, September 11, 2001.

The meeting never took place.

That morning, my phone rang a little before 6:00 a.m. It

was my brother-in-law, his voice filled with urgency, telling me to turn on the television, something terrible was happening. I stumbled over to the living room and turned on the set, in time to see thick plumes of black smoke billowing from the North Tower of the World Trade Center, and people jumping from the windows of the building. At least, that is how I remember the moment. It seems to me now that the television cameras were too far away to have captured the falling bodies, that this was a detail I read about later in a newspaper or a magazine. Yet my memory insists on the detail, as though it were necessary for me to see the individuals in order to apprehend the full scale of the tragedy.

In those days, I thought a lot about memory—how precious it was, and how fragile. The year before the attacks, Alex and I had driven to Orange County, where my mother-in-law had lived since the death of her husband, to celebrate Mother's Day with her. We took her out for lunch on Balboa Island, but throughout the meal, she kept asking us what the name of the island was. Each time we answered, she would say, "¡Oh, sí, verdad!" The following Sunday, when we visited her again, she had forgotten about the lunch altogether. At first, she denied having troubles with memory. She got lost going to the grocery store, but blamed her confusion on a change of landscaping along the avenue. When she stopped making the elaborate meals she usually cooked for us, she insisted it was because she was too tired, not because it was too arduous for her to recall all the steps involved in planning a feast. One time, she withdrew a substantial amount of cash from her bank account and couldn't recall where she put it. Another time, she called the police to say that someone had stolen her wall phone—from inside her house, in a gated community. Later I found the phone, wrapped in its cord, in a cabinet beneath the kitchen counter.

After weeks of cajoling, I managed to get her to see a neurologist, on the promise that I would stay with her and speak to all the nurses myself. The diagnosis hardly came as a surprise: she was showing signs of dementia, probably Alzheimer's disease. Somehow, by repeatedly pressing the point that we couldn't drive thirty-five miles to Orange County every time she needed help, we convinced her to move to a senior residential home five blocks from us in Redondo Beach. The place was in high demand, so she was put on a waitlist. But when her turn finally came up and we went to sign the lease, she abruptly changed her mind. She stood up, throwing her chair back, and screamed that she had no intention of moving out of her house. It was *her* house, no one could steal it from her by forcing her to live elsewhere. The fury in her voice seemed magnified by the slightness of her four-foot-eleven frame.

My mother-in-law and I were very close. Like me, she was a naturalized citizen. She and her husband were both refugees, having come to the United States after the Communist takeover of Cuba and the wave of political repression that followed. "Salimos con nada," she often told me, the implication being "Look what we made of ourselves." Her sons had grown up poor, but one had become an obstetrician and the other an engineer, a living illustration of the American Dream. She opened her heart to me, and treated me as the daughter she never had. We spent many an afternoon together at the movie theater—how she loved the movies!—or at the shopping mall, where I translated for her and in so doing improved my Spanish. Because her birthday fell on Halloween, she often joked that she was a "bruja." Never had a label been so misapplied.

It took a long time, but her paranoia finally receded, giving way to a reluctant acceptance that she was ill. As her memory loss deepened, she became compliant: she agreed to take her pills; she agreed to go to her doctor's appointments; she agreed to have a home aide move in with her in Orange County. A few months into this new arrangement, however, I noticed that a couple of heirlooms had disappeared from her house, and that store receipts didn't match purchases. Of course, I couldn't get any reliable information from her because her short-term memory had become too impaired. Exasperated, we fired the home aide and moved my mother-in-law in with us.

Sometimes, I tried to look at the world through her eyes. All the landmarks she'd once depended on were unrecognizable to her. Each day was new, a blank slate waiting to be filled. When I found an agent for the novel I was writing, she was thrilled, and for weeks I got to break the news to her again and again and watch her face alight with joy each time. Her memory was unreliable, this much she knew by now, and she had to depend on others for tasks big and small, whether it was going to the doctor's or finding her pills in the morning. One day, I went upstairs to take a shower, and when I came back downstairs again she was gone. Perhaps she had decided to go for a walk, but I knew she would never find her way back in an unfamiliar neighborhood. I got in my car and drove around, looking for her, until, in despair, I called the police. A couple of hours later, an officer brought her back in a squad car. Did she agree to get in the car with this stranger because he spoke Spanish? Or was it because he was a figure of authority? I worried constantly about what she might do simply because she was told. Consent had become her natural state.

·   ·   ·

It was during this time of turmoil in my family's life that the attacks of September 11 happened. Driving to work that Tuesday morning, I was waiting at a red light when I saw a man in a T-shirt and jeans take his daughter's hand as they stepped off the curb and crossed the intersection. It was such a small, ordinary gesture—the kind that parents everywhere do multiple times a day. Three hours earlier and three thousand miles away, another man or woman had done the same, at an intersection somewhere in New York. Mothers and fathers and sisters and brothers had sat down to breakfast, finished their coffees, and put on their shoes. I love you, they said. Have a great day. Don't forget to pick up the dry cleaning. Then, one by one, they left home and never came back.

In my memory, the shock and grief of that day are intertwined with fear and rejection. I remember pressing a software engineer on my team about meeting a project deadline, and his response was "What are you going to do? Shoot me? Isn't that how you people solve things?" Only a year earlier, this same co-worker had shared a slice of citizenship apple pie with me. I remember being followed around a home-improvement store while I shopped for flashlights and extension cords for my new home. "What do you need all these cables for?" the clerk asked me at checkout. I remember the pat-downs I received every time I went through an airport.

Because I have light skin, however, these stories rank as inconveniences compared to those of people who are more visibly nonwhite or more conspicuously Muslim. Places of worship, community centers, and businesses were burned down or vandalized; men were killed or assaulted; women were stripped of their headscarves; and children were taunted at school. In the months following the terrorist attacks, hate crimes against

Muslims spiked, accounting for 27 percent of all religious-bias crimes in 2001. Sikh men, frequently mistaken for Muslims because of the turbans they wear, were particularly targeted.

George Bush received a lot of credit in the press for visiting a mosque six days after the attacks and for proclaiming that "the face of terror is not the true faith of Islam," but speaking to a joint session of Congress on September 20, he struck a different tone. He announced that he was launching the War on Terror, which would begin with al-Qaeda, but would not end "until every terrorist group of global reach has been found, stopped, and defeated," an ambition so vast it seemed impossible to shape into concrete, achievable policy. Then he warned that every nation had a decision to make: "Either you are with us or you are with the terrorists." By that point, many countries around the world—including the four whose nationals perpetrated the attacks—had already condemned the terrorists and expressed solidarity with the United States. Americans were more united than ever, and some proudly displayed the flag outside their homes, in their businesses, and even on their cars.

So Bush's pronouncement seemed extraordinary to me, a veiled demand for silent allegiance. Just three days earlier, the comedian Bill Maher had become embroiled in a huge controversy because he had said that, whatever else they were, the terrorists were not cowards; they had stayed in the planes knowing they would die. Advertisers began pulling their support from *Politically Incorrect*, Maher's show on ABC, and some local stations stopped airing it altogether. In *The New Yorker*, Susan Sontag decried the "campaign to infantilize the public" and urged government officials to provide an honest assessment of U.S. intelligence and counter-intelligence failures. This earned her widespread rebuke that lasted for months. "A pretentious buffoon," Andrew Sullivan called her, with no trace of self-awareness. One of the fundamental rights of citizenship—the right to free speech—was being challenged openly.

Seeing powerful white people publicly castigated for daring to dissent made me wonder what might happen to a brown immigrant who was against the impending invasion of Afghanistan. At lunch with a colleague from Human Resources, I expressed serious concerns about the looming war, particularly the toll it would take on innocent civilians already traumatized by decades of conflict. "Well, we didn't do this," she snapped. "They did it to themselves." She gave me a look filled with disbelief and suspicion, as if I had betrayed her by the mere mention of the millions of lives that were at stake while the nation hurtled toward catastrophe. As we drove back to the office, the silence between us was so heavy that I had to turn on the radio. On the news, the history of the United States' interventions in the Middle East—its backing of the Sadat and Mubarak regimes in Egypt, for example, or its alliance with the House of Saud, or its material support of the Mujahideen in Afghanistan—was largely unspoken. From Dick Cheney to Donald Rumsfeld, everyone in the administration was eager to erase a messy and inconvenient past, instead presenting American citizens with the straightforward story of a senseless crime that had to be avenged swiftly.

Bush's message of with-us-or-against-us also carried the implication that one could not be Arab and American, or Muslim and American, unless one was on the side of the United States in its military fights. Opposing the war in Afghanistan and later the war in Iraq—or even casting doubt on their motives and objectives—meant exposing oneself to suspicion. Arab and Muslim citizenship in this country was contingent on either total silence or vocal support for war, a rule that filtered into scripted dramas of the post-9/11 years: along with the usual Muslim terrorists, television series now included the occasional Muslim CIA officer or FBI agent. (The wildly successful Fox series *24*, which premiered in 2001, featured dozens of Arab Muslim terrorists, but by 2005, the Showtime drama *Sleeper Cell* had a black Muslim FBI agent in a starring role.)

The few Muslims invited to opine on national news about the war in Afghanistan and later the war in Iraq—Fareed Zakaria of *Newsweek*, for example, or Fouad Ajami of Johns Hopkins University—were outspoken supporters. Those who opposed the wars, on the other hand, were viewed with distrust, and their allegiance to their country was questioned. When Keith Ellison was elected to represent Minnesota's Fifth District in Congress, on a platform that included ending the Iraq War, Glenn Beck invited him to appear on CNN Headline News and asked him, "Sir, prove to me that you are not working with our enemies."

The demand to prove one's allegiance—even, at times, one's humanity—was made constantly of Arabs and Muslims in those days. When my first book was published, it received critical praise, but it also brought me the experience of hate mail. "What are you?" one reader wrote to me after *USA Today* published an interview with me. "Muslim or human being? It's impossible to be both at the same time." I tried to picture a man going through the trouble of reading the article, looking up my email address, and composing a note telling me that I wasn't human. The charge was so heinous that for days, as I toured the country and signed books, I could think of nothing else. If this American couldn't even see me as a person, there was no chance he would see me as his equal—a citizen of the same nation and with the same rights. *You're either with us, or you're against us.*

Bush's threat was decisive, and it proved popular in the confusing days after September 11, so he returned to it. "Either you are with us," he said later, "or you are with the enemy. There's no in between." My whole life has been lived in-between—in between languages, in between cultures, in between countries. I was a child of the working class, but I went to a private French school. I was a math and science student, but in college I chose to major in English. I had come to the U.S. as a foreign scholar, but later I became an immigrant. My life resisted the kind of easy categories that the head of state had outlined for everyone. Surely, I told myself, a nation was a community, with views that are by necessity different, often divergent, and occasionally contradictory. Surely, true allegiance meant speaking up when something wasn't right.

These were difficult questions, the kind I entertained when I had time to myself, which was not often in those days. In addition to my job and my writing, I helped take care of my mother-in-law at home. Sometimes, she was quiet and cheerful, whispering "Thank you" after we got her dressed or drove her to her bingo game at the community center or took her to get her hair and nails done. Other times, when she was having a bad day, she would threaten to leave or hint at dangerous enemies or demand to see Maria. (Maria was her mother, who died in 1986.) Dementia made her stubborn, and if she settled on a particular request or recrimination, it could take hours to distract her from it. But what never changed, throughout the excruciating years of her mental decline, was the love between us, built on a commitment that her circumstances could never change.

By 2007, when a little-known senator from Illinois with the middle name Hussein announced his presidential candidacy, I thought the odds of his victory were remote. The campaign was bitterly fought, both between Barack Obama and Hillary Clinton for the Democratic nomination, and later between Barack Obama and John McCain for the presidency, but to this day one exchange remains indelible in my mind. During a town hall in Lakeville, Minnesota, which was shown on CNN in October 2008, a white woman told McCain that "I can't trust Obama. I have read about him, and he's not, he's not, he's a—an Arab." "No, ma'am," McCain replied, taking away her microphone. "He's a decent family man, a citizen that I just happen to have disagreements with on fundamental issues."

I was lying on the rug in our living room, playing dominoes with our toddler, but the word *citizen* made me sit up in disbelief. "Did you hear that?" I asked my husband. The conversation on CNN highlighted two contradictions, which remained unchallenged for the rest of the telecast. The first was a contradiction between being "an Arab" and being "a decent family man." The woman said Obama couldn't be trusted because he was an Arab, and the rebuttal wasn't about the lack of causality between the two; it was a reassurance that he wasn't Arab, he was a family man. The second contradiction was between being "an Arab" and being "a citizen." Clearly, Obama could only be the latter if he was not the former. But even McCain's questionable defense was not enough for the people who attended his town hall: when he reassured them that they need not be scared of an Obama presidency, they booed.

The conspiracy theory about Obama's citizenship, which started as early as 2004 and outlasted his presidency, was resistant to factual corrections. It didn't matter that Obama released both a short-form certificate and a long-form certificate from the state of Hawaii: there was always an alternate explanation. Birthers, as they came to be called, would claim that the documents had been forged, or that Obama had relinquished his citizenship when he lived in Indonesia as a child. At one point, as many as 25 percent of Americans believed the lie, and solid majorities of Republicans and Southerners did. The rumor continued to spread on email chains and social media, and was promoted by talk-show hosts like Michael Savage, celebrities like Chuck Norris, and John McCain's own running mate, Sarah Palin.

The birther theory was nearly always paired with rumors that Obama was a Kenyan Marxist and a secret Muslim. This is significant because it exemplifies how race and religion are conditions of citizenship in America. In attributing Kenyan-ness and Muslim-ness to Obama, right-wing pundits were exploiting implicitly held notions about who gets to be American. They were also substituting themselves for agents of the state: they wanted him to show them his papers, and, when the papers were finally produced, dismissed them as fake. A white candidate, it goes without saying, would not have been asked these questions. In a sense, Obama, too, was caught in between. He had to prove his Americanness by showing his birth certificate; publicly declaring his Christianity; distancing himself from Rashid Khalidi, the Columbia professor and advocate for Palestinian rights; and denouncing Jeremiah Wright, the pastor who in the wake of 9/11 had sharply criticized U.S. foreign policy and its blowback effects. Obama went to great lengths to show his love—and gratitude—for the U.S. "In no other country in the world is my story even possible," he often said.

Although Obama had been elected on a promise that he would end the conflicts in Iraq and Afghanistan, his expansion of the War on Terror to new fronts in Pakistan, Yemen, and Syria drew scant protests. Compliance had become normal. The prevailing response within his own party seemed to be that since he was relying primarily on airstrikes or drone strikes, rather than deploying tens of thousands of new troops on the ground, his approach was better than that of his predecessor. (He himself told the few Senate Democrats who challenged him on the legal justification for his use of drones in 2013, "This is not Dick Cheney we're talking about here." Well, then.) In addition, many Democrats refused to be too vocal in their opposition to him precisely because of the racist attacks from Republicans on his person, his family, and his citizenship.

One of the complicating factors for Obama's presidency is that many white people saw in him only figments of their imagination. White liberals treated him like another Martin Luther King, Jr., a savior who would deliver the nation from any and all ills. Shepard Fairey's *Hope* poster is perhaps the purest expression of this view. White conservatives, meanwhile, thought of him as a young Malcolm X, a radical who would never compromise on anything. The widely circulated picture of Obama in a turban and traditional dress while he was on a visit to Kenya reinforced this notion. Neither perspective quite captured the fact that Obama was first and foremost a skilled politician, successful at the art of the possible.

Perhaps the most famous promoter of the birther theory was the man who became the next president of the United States: Donald Trump. As candidate, Trump's most prominent policy promises were the building of a border wall along the entire southern border and a ban on Muslims entering the country. The ban was staked on the idea that Muslims did not belong in the United States, that they were unwanted latecomers who were trying to graft themselves onto a thriving Judeo-Christian nation. This is a political position that derives from the erasure of Muslims from America's collective past, which makes them invisible in the present, and justifies policies against them.

But at no point during his campaign did Trump have to answer questions about his Americanness or show his gratitude to his country. On the contrary, he called America "foolish," "dumb," "very, very stupid," and "the laughing stock of the world." The United States was "going to hell," it looked "like a third world country," and frankly it was "an embarrassment." All this and more he could say, because, unlike Obama, he enjoyed the full rights of citizenship, including the freedom to express himself without fear of having his allegiance called into question.

After he was sworn into office, Trump began implementing his campaign promises, beginning with an immigration ban on Muslims. The executive order faced immediate and successful challenges in federal courts because it was so plainly inconsistent with the Establishment Clause of the First Amendment. While court appeals were still in progress, Rudy Giuliani, the president's lawyer, admitted in a Fox News interview that Trump had called him and said, "Show me the right way to do it legally." It would take the president a few months and two revisions in order to figure this out, but in September 2017, he signed a presidential proclamation that banned North Koreans and Venezuelan government officials from entering the U.S., along with all nationals of Syria, Iran, Libya, Somalia, and Yemen.

This was a deceitful move, because the government of North Korea already prevents its people from leaving their homeland and only about forty Venezuelan officials visit the United States per year. By contrast, the State Department issued well over 70,000 visas in 2016 to nationals from the Muslim countries on the list. But the deception provided enough plausible deniability for the conservative justices on the Supreme Court, who, in an opinion written by John Roberts, ruled that the president's well-documented animus toward Muslims was "extrinsic" to the issue and that the ban was "facially neutral toward religion." With this precedent, the president can add more Muslim countries to the list, without serious risk of constitutional challenge.

The Muslim ban seemingly applies only to foreigners. For this reason, and despite initial opposition from liberals and progressives, it has largely faded from the news. But in reality, the ban affects millions of Americans directly. An Iranian-American in Los Angeles can no longer sponsor his mother for a visa, but a German-American can. A Libyan-American in Ann Arbor can no longer receive a visit from her grandfather, but an Italian-American can. A Yemeni-American in New York can no longer bring a relative to the city for medical treatment, but a Portuguese-American can. In other words, what Trump effectively did, and with direct approval from the Supreme Court, was codify American Muslims' conditional citizenship into law.

Conditional citizenship is not unique to Muslims in America. Millions of people in this country live with the terrible reality that their relationship to the state is at least partly determined by the color of their skin, the nature of their creed, their gender identity, or their national origin. American citizenship was created in the image of the man who wrote the Declaration of Independence: it was a status reserved for "free white persons," with some rights—like the right to vote—further restricted to white, male landowners. Rich white men were to be governed by consent, and everyone else was to be governed by force. It took centuries of struggle, some of it violent and bloody, for this philosophy to be disrupted, but it has not yet been fully dismantled. The groups that have been historically denied the rights and privileges of citizenship in the United States are still today struggling to achieve equal civil rights, equal access to the vote, and an equal sense of belonging to the American family. Conditional citizenship manifests itself in many different ways, some plain and others subtle, and with varying degrees of violence.

Conditional citizens are people whose rights the state finds expendable in the pursuit of white supremacy. Between 1778 and 1871, for instance, the U.S. government signed hundreds of treaties with indigenous tribes, treaties that were meant to last "as long as water flows, or grass grows upon the earth, or the sun rises to show your pathway." But these agreements were summarily abrogated whenever the government decided it wanted indigenous land for gold, oil, or colonial settlement that, by and large, profited white citizens or white immigrants. As recently as two years ago, the Standing Rock Sioux Tribe fought to stop the building of an oil pipeline that could pollute water on its reservation, in violation of a previous treaty that guaranteed it sovereignty and undisturbed use of the land. Native communities across the United States still face land loss and a slew of challenges to their individual and collective rights.

The proverbial "forty acres and a mule" serves as another example of a contract broken by the state. In January 1865, after a meeting with black ministers and activists in Savannah, General William Tecumseh Sherman issued a special field order setting aside forty acres of land each to newly freed slaves in Georgia, South Carolina, and Florida. In total, the land grant redistributed 400,000 acres that had been previously owned by Confederate planters. Sherman later ordered the army to lend black settlers a mule with which to work the land. Within weeks, tens of thousands of formerly enslaved families had taken advantage of the grant. By the fall of 1865, however, President Andrew Johnson overturned the order. The federal government gave the land back to the very people who had mounted a rebellion against it, and the former slaves were, once again, dispossessed. Since then, reparations have often been debated—most recently when a House Judiciary Committee held a hearing on the subject—but always denied.

Conditional citizens are policed and punished more harshly than others by the state. For example, African-Americans are incarcerated five times more often than white people, and Hispanics two times more often. The high rate of incarceration among nonwhites derives principally from the so-called "war on drugs," which was launched by Richard Nixon in 1971, and escalated by successive administrations. Although whites and nonwhites use drugs at roughly the same rates, the criminalization of drug use among nonwhites has resulted in the creation of the largest prison system in the world. In her book *The New Jim Crow*, Michelle Alexander showed persuasively that mass incarceration in America functions as a system of "racial hierarchy and control." This racially based punitive system is so pervasive and so internalized that policing begins in childhood. A black child who becomes involved in a school infraction is statistically more likely to be given suspension than a white child.

Conditional citizens are not guaranteed the same electoral representation as others. Historically, the right to vote in the United States has been restricted in many different ways, with race, class, gender, and religion serving as constraints on suffrage. These were loosened incrementally over a period of two hundred years, but new restrictions were imposed, such as literacy, poll taxes, or assimilation into white society. Today, voting rights are still being contested, with the result that the fruits of democracy are not available equally to all. The voter ID laws that have been passed in more than a dozen states over the last two decades have disproportionately affected black, Hispanic, and indigenous voters, resulting in flagrant voter suppression. Four years ago, the Fourth Circuit Court of Appeals ruled that North Carolina's voter-identification law was designed to "target African-Americans with almost surgical precision." Yet such laws continue to be passed in state legislatures.

Conditional citizens are more likely to be expatriated or denaturalized. Although both expatriation and denaturalization remain unusual, they tend to be used against marginalized groups. For example, the Expatriation Act of 1907 stripped American women who had married a foreigner of their citizenship, under the view that their matrimonial choices made them disloyal to their country. In addition to losing their right to a passport, these women also lost the right to work for the government. During the First World War, American women who married German immigrants had to register as enemy aliens. Congress passed legislation in the 1920s to allow U.S.-born women to keep their nationality if they married foreign men who were eligible for citizenship—typically, white immigrants from Europe—but the law didn't effectively give women the same permanent right to citizenship until the 1940s.

Because citizenship and race are historically linked, denaturalization often targets nonwhites. This is what happened to Bhagat Singh Thind, an Indian-born writer and U.S. Army veteran who was denaturalized four days after being granted citizenship in 1923. Despite his appeal that he was both "Aryan" and "Caucasian," and therefore eligible for citizenship by any reasonable definition of "free white person," the Supreme Court ruled against him. After this decision, the government moved to denaturalize all Indian-born citizens it could find. Naturalization would only become available to nonwhite immigrants, regardless of national origin, after the Immigration Act of 1965.

Broadly speaking, denaturalization is a rare process, with just a few dozen cases spread out over several decades, but it has the potential to become systematic. In 2009, the Obama administration started an investigative program called Operation Janus, which uncovered cases where biographic data in citizenship applications didn't match data in federal databases. This resulted in accusations of fraud and denaturalization proceedings against some sixteen hundred individuals. By the summer of 2018, the Trump administration announced that it would expand this program into a Denaturalization Task Force, housed in a special office in Southern California. The operation is ostensibly aimed at fraudulent cases only, but the publicity that surrounds its existence casts a pall of fear over the lives of naturalized citizens, making it clear to them that they cannot take their status in America for granted.

Conditional citizens are surveilled more closely by the state. I don't just mean the additional scrutiny that some people are subjected to at ports of entry at the discretion of Customs and Border Protection officers, but specific surveillance programs aimed at entire populations of unsuspecting citizens. In 2002, the New York Police Department established a secret office, innocuously called the Demographics Unit, with the sole purpose of spying on Muslims in the city and surrounding suburbs. The unit placed informants in mosques, infiltrated student groups, eavesdropped on customers at Muslim-owned businesses, gained access to private homes by means of subterfuge, and created vast databases of information. But in six years of warrantless surveillance—and violation of the civil rights of New York Muslims—the unit did not generate a single lead.

In short, conditional citizens are Americans who cannot

enjoy the full rights, liberties, and protections of citizenship because of arbitrary markers of identity. Their race, ethnicity, gender, and national origin—that is to say, features over which they have no control—largely determine whether they will be able to vote, have freedom of movement, or remain safe from unreasonable searches. To say that millions of people in the United States are conditional citizens is not to say that their experiences with discrimination or exclusion are identical; it is merely to observe the ways in which their rights are curtailed or violated, with the result that a caste system is maintained, keeping the modern equivalent of white male landowners at the top of the social hierarchy.

The existing limitations to citizenship stand in sharp contrast to the civic ideals that Americans are taught. Every morning in this country, schoolchildren recite a pledge of allegiance that promises them one nation under God, indivisible, with liberty and justice for all. Then they grow up to find that, depending on the lottery of their birth, the state might actively or passively deny them equal status, equal participation in the electoral process, equal rights, or an equal sense of belonging in the community. Conditional citizens are people who know what it is like for a country to embrace you with one arm, and push you away with the other.

Yet I am still here. When I arrived in the United States as a foreign student, I had no idea that someday it would become my home. I fell in love with America at the same time as I fell in love with an American. We have spent more than twenty years together, sharing good times and bad. During those years, my mother-in-law slowly forgot how to dress, how to bathe, how to talk, and even how to eat. She forgot her husband, her siblings, her children, and me. By the end of her life, we lived on the periphery of her consciousness, occasional visitors whose faces no longer stirred feelings of recognition. But until her death, the love was there. I could still see it in her eyes, sometimes. Love is powerful. Love is honest. It is because I love America that I cannot be quiet about her faults. The price of my belonging cannot be my silence.

The Pomona Fairplex, where I took the oath of allegiance, is still used for citizenship ceremonies. But the site once served a different purpose. During the Second World War, it operated as an assembly center for Japanese-Americans—citizens whom the state had designated a danger to national security through an executive order. Beginning on May 9, 1942, Japanese families from Los Angeles, San Francisco, and Santa Clara counties were told to report to the Fairplex, a directive that the *Los Angeles Times* covered in a brief article the next day with the headline "Aliens to Go to Pomona." There, they were housed in barracks hastily built by the Army Corps of Engineers, forced to live under curfew, and watched over by a team of white policemen. In August, they were taken by train to the Heart Mountain concentration camp in Wyoming, where they were held without charge until the end of the war.

The row of barracks at the Fairplex is now a parking lot. I don't think the erasure is accidental. Over the last twenty years, I have come to understand that there is nothing more American than forgetting the past. It is through the obliteration of memory, an obliteration perpetrated with great deliberation by the state upon the citizenry, that American identity is fashioned. But conditional citizens will insist on remembering. In August 2016, a group of Japanese-Americans convinced the Fairplex to install a brass plaque at the site of internment. It reads "May such injustice and suffering never recur."

Faith

In the spring of 2015, I gave a reading from my third novel, *The Moor's Account,* to a literary organization in Arizona. The event took place over lunch in the ballroom of an upscale hotel, and the mood, especially after wine was served, was warm and congenial. During the discussion that followed my presentation, a white woman in a blue pantsuit asked me to talk about my upbringing in Morocco. It is only natural for readers to want to know more about writers, I told myself; they're curious about the kinds of circumstances that lead some people to a creative life. I continued to tell myself this even after the subsequent questions drifted from Morocco to Islam—and then to ISIS.

I wish I could say that it was unusual for me to field questions about terrorist groups at an event that was, at least ostensibly, about historical fiction. *The Moor's Account* is based on the true story of an enslaved man who was one of the first outsiders to travel across America in the early sixteenth century. This man, called Estebanico by Spanish conquistadors and Mustafa in my novel, was from the village of Azamor on the Atlantic coast, about a hundred miles from where I was born nearly five hundred years later. I was drawn to his story because it combined elements of adventure, survival, and reinvention: between his landing in Florida in 1528 and his arrival in Mexico in 1536, he transformed himself several times, from slave to refugee to shamanic leader. Yet the journey of the protagonist and the life of the author somehow seemed to trigger, in this woman's mind, some connection to terrorism.

As I answered, I felt keenly the gaze of people in the audience, a gaze I would describe as filled with wonder—it was as if I were a rare species of human they had not encountered before. Then another woman, a redhead in fashionable glasses, raised her hand and said that the only Muslims she saw when she turned on the television were extremists. "Why aren't we hearing from people like you?" she asked me. "You are," I said with a nervous laugh. "Right now." But any private exasperation I might have felt at being asked about ISIS vanished. What I understood this second woman to be saying was that the media she consumed had not provided her with enough context with which to interpret current events, so she didn't know how to process the fact that the Muslim at the dais didn't match the Muslim on television.

Having to explain this mismatch is not a task I chose for myself, but from the moment I moved to the United States, it was asked of me with disturbing regularity. How often have I seen disbelief fall across people's faces when they asked where I was from and, a minute later, realized from my answer that I was Muslim! Immediately the questions would come pouring forth, questions about the veil, or the fatwa, or even, as was the case with this reader in Arizona, ISIS. The wide abyss between the imagined me and the real me had the paradoxical effect of making my life narrower, because if I spent my time correcting misconceptions about the Muslim community, then I was left with little opportunity to engage with issues that mattered to me within that community.

.   .   .

This dynamic leaves no room for complicated stories like my family's, which begin to seem unusual because they are so rarely heard. My mother was born in 1941, when Morocco was still under French colonial rule, and orphaned as a child; she has no memory of when or how her parents died, an amnesia that, I suspect, was caused by trauma. Somehow, she found herself in a French orphanage run by Franciscan nuns in Fes. Growing up, she was taught to pray to Jesus and the Virgin Mary, attend mass on Sunday, and wear a uniform to school. From the age of seven onward, she also had to do needlework, and the result of her and her classmates' labor—tablecloths, napkins, bridal trousseaus—was sold to support the orphanage. In 1956, after Morocco gained its independence from French rule, the nuns abruptly told their charges that they had to practice their own religion now.

Just like that. One moment you're in this religion, the next you're in another. If the change required a radical rethinking of the self, however, it was not the case for my mother. Perhaps her daily exposure to the Moroccan staff who worked in the kitchen, at the laundry, or on the grounds, all of them Muslim, lessened the confusion over the next few years. Or perhaps her relationship to older girls who had come to the orphanage in their teens, and had been keeping the Ramadan fast in secret, made the transition easier. Still, for the rest of her life, my mother never lost her connection to Catholicism: she wore an Our Lady of Lourdes pendant sometimes, said a prayer to St. Anthony when she misplaced something, and stored her sewing kit in a metal box bearing the likeness of the Virgin Mary.

My father met my mother through an arranged "coffee date" organized by the Franciscan nuns. A year later, they married and she moved with him to the capital of Rabat, where they lived first with my grandparents, then in an apartment a few miles away, and finally in their own home in the suburbs. Although my mother now identified as Muslim, she still maintained her social relationships with the nuns who raised her. I remember going with her to have tea with Sister Gisèle, who was working at Notre Dame de la Paix care center in Rabat in the late 1970s. "Only one cookie," my mother would tell me before we went in. "Don't ask for another, it's rude." Not only did I know many Christians personally, like Sister Gisèle and some of the teachers at my school, they were also present to me imaginatively, in all the books I read—from *Tintin* to *Twenty Thousand Leagues Under the Sea,* and from *The Count of Monte Cristo* to *Tartuffe.*

My paternal grandmother, with whom I spent a great deal of time as a child, was born in a small town sixty miles north of Marrakesh. After she married my grandfather, she moved with him to Rabat, where he was posted as a police brigadier. In a family portrait taken in 1948, my grandfather sits in a chair, wearing a dark-colored jellaba and a tarbush, while she stands beside him, her face uncovered, her hair pulled back in a crocheted kerchief. Around them stand five of their nine children, all of them dressed in European clothes. This picture hung above the fireplace in my grandparents' house; it was not meant to be seen outside of it. In keeping with tradition, my grandmother lived cloistered in her home, leaving it only to go to the bathhouse, or the doctor, or to visit her relations. However, after my grandfather died in 1969, she suddenly found herself in charge of his finances, and had to go out to meet or negotiate with tenants at a couple of rental properties he owned. She did this successfully in spite of severe educational limitations—she was illiterate.

My grandmother was a practicing Muslim. She prayed every day, kept the fast in Ramadan, gave alms to the poor, and saved money for years in order to go on the pilgrimage to Mecca. What she taught me about faith was through example: she dressed modestly, but didn't offer opinions about my mother's short skirts; she carried her prayer beads, but didn't object to the Catholic imagery that appeared from time to time in our home. If she was staying with us when one of the nuns visited, she cooked one of her delicious tagines for them. From my mother and grandmother, I learned about faith as a private relationship with the cosmic, which did not need to be measured by adherence to strict rules and rituals. This faith stood in sharp contrast to religion, at least as it came into my life once I started middle school. All of a sudden, I couldn't be seen with boys who weren't my schoolmates. In religious education classes, I was taught that men have authority over women and served as their guardians. This was why men could inherit more, could divorce at will, and could marry outside of their faith, while women couldn't. Religion, unlike faith, emphasized strict adherence to texts, and failure to abide by them was perceived as a moral failure.

Still, in those days, the political mood favored secular pan-Arabism, with Gamal Abdel-Nasser frequently coming up in the adults' conversations around me. It was the height of the Cold War, and many Arab leaders were punished or rewarded by world powers depending on whether they aligned with the Soviet Union or the United States. In the case of Morocco, this meant that France and the United States propped up King Hassan, their strategic ally, even as he arrogated to himself vast constitutional powers, assassinated the left-wing leader

Mehdi Ben Barka, survived two coup d'état attempts by the military, and engaged in an extensive campaign of disappearance, imprisonment, and torture against leftist opponents, journalists, and student protesters. (This wave of repression, which ran from the 1960s to the 1980s, would later come to be known as the Years of Lead.) As a counterbalance to the criticism of his rule, which came principally from the secular left, the king gave wide latitude to the religious right. What happened next was predictable: by the late 1980s, religious rhetoric became one of the few outlets through which to express political dissent.

Along with these political changes, there were cultural changes as well. Television programming, which had been available exclusively on the state channel, was massively expanded when satellite dishes appeared on the market. Overnight, hundreds of foreign channels became available. I remember standing on the roof terrace of my best friend's house and being struck by the sea of satellite dishes below me, stretching as far as the eye could see. In our country, the dominant school of Islamic jurisprudence was the Maliki school, but now live programming from the Middle East brought access to others, including the Hanbali school and its associated doctrines, the strictly traditionalist Wahhabi and Salafi movements. Meanwhile, the regime continued to stifle dissent, while encouraging, and eventually trying to co-opt, religious conservatives. The king's celebration of religious holidays— Ramadan, for example—became more ostentatious. Within a few years, a new social conservatism began to take root in Morocco. In middle school, I had known only one girl who wore the headscarf, but by the time I finished high school, there were several in my graduating class. Two of my classmates, once infamous for their partying, began attending prayers at the neighborhood mosque.

Yet for all these cultural changes, the concerns of everyone around me continued to be prosaic: periodic and increasingly severe droughts had forced a great number of people to migrate from rural to urban areas, stretching poorly functioning social services. Rents were skyrocketing, classrooms were packed, hospital care was deteriorating. All these factors raised hopes for *alternance*, a policy proposed by King Hassan, which would allow opposition parties to finally exercise political power. The 1997 elections led to two significant developments: the appointment as prime minister of Abderrahman Youssoufi, one of the few remaining socialist leaders from the old era, and the election of the first Islamist representatives to Parliament. Left and right now had a voice in government, though it continued to serve at the pleasure of the king.

By this time, I had moved to the United States, but whenever I traveled back to Morocco, I heard the same complaints: high rates of unemployment among college graduates; poor quality of public education and public healthcare; endemic corruption in government institutions; and persistent human rights abuses. Even in my limited interactions with agents of the state, little seemed to have changed. One time, I remember, when my husband and I were on holiday near Tetuan, a police officer stopped us for a minor traffic violation and asked for a bribe to let us go. (I managed to talk the officer out of it.) Another time, when my father had an emergency procedure at Avicenna Hospital in Rabat, I was stunned to find that an entire surgical wing continued to operate even as construction was being completed outside.

What did this complex history, whether private or public, have to do with ISIS? What special insight did the woman in the blue pantsuit expect me to have about it? My being Arab and Muslim seemed to grant me, at least in her eyes, some kind of expertise on the subject of a recently formed transnational terrorist group that combined Islamist ideology with traditional guerrilla tactics. I had lived my life in the singular, yet she wanted me to talk about it in the representative—to explain, to clarify, to contextualize everything that she didn't know or understand about ISIS.

If Muslims seemed that strange or exotic to her, it was presumably because she was unaware that they had been part of America since before the founding of the United States. The earliest Muslims to land in North America arrived here with Spanish expeditions in the early sixteenth century, long before there was a colony at Jamestown. As many as thirty percent of enslaved people who were brought over the next two centuries were Muslims from West Africa, who were forcibly converted and given new names.

In addition to the enslaved man known as Estebanico, who landed in Florida in 1528, a number of Muslims left their mark on American history. For instance, one of the earliest slave narratives in this country comes from Ayuba Suleiman Diallo, also known as Job Ben Solomon, a slave merchant from Bundu, in present-day Senegal, who was himself captured in 1730 and brought to Maryland. Another important narrative was the work of Omar ibn Said, a Senegalese religious scholar who was kidnapped, sold into slavery in 1807, and brought to South Carolina. Unlike Diallo, whose story was told through an interpreter and edited by a British judge, ibn Said composed his memoir in Arabic, in the Maghribi script. "I reside in this country by reason of great necessity," he wrote. "Wicked men took me by violence & sold me to the Christians." Two more narratives of American slavery were left behind by Abdulrahman ibn Ibrahima, a Fulani nobleman who was enslaved in his native Guinea and spent forty years in bondage. Finally, in 1828, a letter he wrote found its way to the sultan of Morocco, who petitioned John Quincy Adams for his release.

I know of no written narratives by the hundreds of thousands of enslaved Muslim women who survived the march to the African coast, the Middle Passage, and the torture and brutality—physical, sexual, and psychological—of colonial plantations. The historical record preserved their lives and deaths only as commodities, as lines in sale and transfer ledgers, never as human stories, with names and pasts and hopes and desires and fears. Bondage erased all that made them individuals, prevented them from preserving their cultural heritage, and made it impossible for them to practice or pass down their religions. By 1936, when the Federal Writers' Project began collecting oral narratives from the last surviving formerly enslaved people, there was no trace of Muslim identity left.

With one possible exception. A woman baptized Silvia King, who had the "appearance of extreme age," said she had been born "in Morocco, in Africa, and was married and had children befor' I was stoled from my husband." She was drugged, taken to France, and thereafter transported to New Orleans. Although birth in Morocco does not by itself establish a specific religious identity, it remains likely that Silvia King was born Muslim. Some scholars have also argued that the poet Phillis Wheatley, who in 1773 became the first African-American woman to publish a collection of poetry, already knew the Arabic alphabet when she arrived in Boston and might have been a Muslim from Gambia or Senegal.

On the whole, however, maintaining familial, cultural, or

religious traditions under conditions of slavery was impossible. For this reason, the first mosque established in this country was not built by enslaved or formerly enslaved men and women, but by immigrants who arrived three centuries later. In 1929, Syrian and Lebanese homesteaders built a masjid in Ross, North Dakota, a structure that still exists today.

Since the history of Muslims in this country is characterized by erasure, fiction often presents one of the few opportunities to learn about them or their faith. Yet when I considered this other possibility, I realized that the woman in the blue pantsuit might not have grown up reading stories about Muslim characters either. Novels like the *Cairo Trilogy,* or *For Bread Alone,* or *So Long a Letter* are not widely taught in American schools. The books about Muslims most likely to be stocked in her chain bookstore were reportage on current events in the Middle East or else polemics about Muslim immigration. The previous Christmas, her local movie theater had almost certainly shown the blockbuster *American Sniper*, a movie that presented Muslims as little more than savages. Living in Arizona, this woman might not have had many acquaintances or neighbors or teachers who were Muslim and she probably hadn't lived or traveled extensively in Muslim countries. She asked about ISIS because she didn't know much about it—a perfectly reasonable thing to do.

The woman appeared to be in her sixties, however. Over the course of her lifetime, the United States had dropped bombs or fought wars in Lebanon, Libya, Kuwait, Iraq, Afghanistan, Somalia, Pakistan, Yemen, Syria, and Sudan, and had troops stationed in Saudi Arabia, Qatar, Djibouti, Niger, and Nigeria. Yet despite half a century of intervention in Muslim-majority countries—and interruption of their political destinies—this woman was still confused about ISIS. The hegemony that her country exercised gave her the privilege of being ignorant about other nations, other peoples, other faiths. It was as though she lived in a garden of innocence, removed from the knowledge that ought to come with being a citizen of the United States, until I appeared on the dais with an apple.

The Islamic State in Iraq and Syria—commonly referred to with the acronym ISIS—was founded by a Jordanian national named Ahmed Fadhil al-Nazal al-Khalaylah. Born in 1966 in the town of Zarqa, northeast of Amman, al-Khalaylah dropped out of high school and got into drunken brawls, seemingly destined for a life of petty crime. Sometime in the late 1980s, however, he decided to travel to Afghanistan to join the Mujahideen in their struggle against the Soviet occupation. (At the time, the Mujahideen received financial and material support from the Reagan administration.) Whether he saw much combat remains unclear, but he met and befriended others who had been fighting the Soviets. At the end of the war in Afghanistan, he returned to Jordan, where he tried to organize a new group of militants against the regime of King Hussein.

In the United States, the king of Jordan—like the king of Morocco—enjoyed a reputation as an important ally and an enlightened ruler. Yet his reign, which lasted more than four decades, was characterized by repression and turbulence. He banned political parties in 1957, lost control of Jerusalem in the 1967 war with Israel, and faced serious challenges from the Palestinian Fedayeen, whom he defeated during the bloody fighting of Black September. Because he ruled under martial law, there was little room for political dissent in his country. But in 1989, protests that had broken out over the rising cost of gasoline and other necessities turned political, which finally led King Hussein to lift martial law and allow elections. It was at about this time that Ahmed al-Khalaylah returned to Jordan and formed a militant group, known as Jund al-Sham. He was arrested and sent to prison, then was released in 1999 as part of an amnesty deal.

Al-Khalaylah was reportedly undeterred by his stint in jail. In 2001, after the United States invaded Afghanistan, he traveled back to the region, where he set up a training camp and formed alliances with Osama bin Laden and his Sunni Islamist terror organization, al-Qaeda. Two years later, when George W. Bush started another war in Iraq, al-Khalaylah moved to this new battleground to fight the occupiers. By this point, he had taken on the nom de guerre Abu Musab al-Zarqawi, naming himself after his hometown of Zarqa. Although he had formally pledged allegiance to al-Qaeda, he deployed new tactics in the Iraq war: his group fought American troops as well as Shia-affiliated militants, contributing to extreme and violent sectarianism in the country. The Bush administration's decision to disband the Iraqi army shortly after the invasion and to ban members of the Baath Party from positions of influence made matters significantly worse: thousands of Iraqis, many with military training, were left with no jobs, no income, and no prospects. These men constituted easy recruits for different insurgent groups fighting against the U.S. occupation in Iraq.

It is impossible to tell the story of ISIS without reference to Arab dictators or American presidents. Tyrants, terrorists, invaders, and occupiers—each played a part in what happened in Iraq and Syria. But this story leaves out ordinary people, who had to live through the upheavals of war, displacement, and authoritarianism. Although al-Zarqawi was killed in a U.S. strike in 2006, the group he founded—al-Qaeda in Iraq—survived him, rebranded itself the Islamic State, and, under the leadership of a series of commanders, gained territory in Iraq incrementally. In 2011, after a popular uprising against the regime of Bashar al-Assad turned into a civil war, ISIS gained a foothold in Syria, establishing its capital in the city of Raqqa for four years. The people of Raqqa had to obey laws that ranged from the horrifying to the absurd: the heads of prisoners who were executed were posted on spikes in the town's main square; women had to wear a niqab and be accompanied by a male companion when they went out; smoking and swearing were not allowed; chemistry was no longer taught in schools; and traffic police were not permitted to have whistles because ISIS considered them un-Islamic.

The people of Raqqa did not control their political destinies—they lived under a terror regime that was being bombed by the Syrian armed forces, with support from several foreign militaries—but my audience in Arizona could, at least in principle, hold its government to account. As citizens of the United States, the Americans in that upscale hotel ballroom could freely vote for, or vote out, any leaders they wanted. So it seemed to me not irrelevant that George W. Bush, the man who decided to invade Afghanistan in 2001 and Iraq in 2003, won the state of Arizona, as well as re-election to the presidency, in 2004.

I wondered if this was the response that the woman in the blue pantsuit wanted from me: a broad outline of how ISIS was founded, how it grew to become an international threat, and the role that U.S. invasions played in its inception. But if that was the case, then it would have been fairly easy for her to find this information. After all, in the spring of 2015, ISIS was covered almost daily in American newspapers, on the radio, and on television. Debates and controversies about how to respond to the increasingly vicious attacks by ISIS consumed much of the media coverage. The year before, Barack Obama had drawn the ire of Republicans when he'd called ISIS the "jayvee team" of terrorists. A year later, Donald Trump would blame him for the founding of the organization and, when confronted about these comments, respond with "I meant he's the founder of ISIS. The way he got out of Iraq, that was the founding of ISIS."

Perhaps the soundbites, controversies, and partisan blame were exactly what made it so hard for this woman to learn more about ISIS. On cable news, for example, contributors who are invited to comment on foreign policy issues are often surrogates for political campaigns. This woman may have wanted to hear from someone who was not involved in electoral politics and had no agenda to sell. Yet there was plenty of reportage in the United States on ISIS. Several national newspapers— the *New York Times*, the *Washington Post*, and the *Los Angeles Times,* to name just three—had correspondents on the ground who wrote about the terrorist group's actions in Iraq and Syria, sometimes at great risk to themselves. Was it really so hard for her to inform herself that she had to ask me, "Could you talk to us about ISIS?"

Being asked about ISIS at a literary reading didn't offend or enrage me; those were my reactions the first few times it happened. By the time I was asked it in Arizona, however, I was merely tired. If the guest at the dais had been a white writer, invited to talk about a novel of exploration set in sixteenth-century America, would any of the readers in attendance have brought up the KKK? After all, the KKK is a terrorist organization that, like ISIS, seeks a mythical purity—racial in the case of the KKK and religious in the case of ISIS. Both groups find inspiration in their holy books to justify the use of violence against others. And both groups have received quiet support, whether financial or material, from sympathizers in high places, including members of governments. Just three months after my event in Arizona, a twenty-one-year-old white supremacist named Dylann Roof walked into the Emanuel African Methodist Episcopal Church in Charleston, South Carolina, and killed nine of the congregants. (It was, for a few years at least, the deadliest mass shooting at a place of worship in the United States.) I tried to imagine an American audience—of any race—asking a white writer who had come to discuss a recently published novel to talk to them about Dylann Roof or other white supremacists.

If the idea of asking a white writer such a question seems laughable, it is simply because to most of these readers, a white writer was an individual, responsible only for his or her own creative work, whereas I was a specimen, culled from a group of people these readers found mysterious and perhaps dangerous. The information I gave—an abbreviated form of what I have included here—was not particularly difficult to find. Yet as a (white) citizen of the United States, the woman in the blue pantsuit had the luxury of being ignorant about a group that grew, at least in part, out of her country's invasion of Iraq. It was a luxury I didn't have.

Muslim Americans who appear in a public forum will, sooner or later, face the question of terrorism. It doesn't matter if the forum is a literary event or a fashion show or the floor of Congress, the question will come up. It may take the form of an accusation, from someone who has been fed a diet of propaganda, or it may take the form of a sincere remark. It may even take the form of a joke, intended to lighten the mood of the audience. But it will come. And when it does, the Muslim

faces an impossible choice: ignore the comment and perpetuate the association with terrorism or address the comment and
perpetuate the association anyway. There is no right answer.
There is only the hope, by speaking about oneself, to create
room for idiosyncrasy. Conditional citizenship is characterized
by the burden of having to educate white Americans about all
the ways in which one is different from them.

Like other terrorist groups before it, ISIS depends on publicity for recruitment and survival. As part of its efforts to spread
its message around the world, the organization used to put
out an English-language magazine, called *Dabiq*. In February 2015, a month before my event in Arizona, *Dabiq* published a twelve-page article, with high-resolution photos and
multiple footnotes, cheering the terrorist attacks of September 11 and claiming that they made manifest for the world two
camps: the camp of Islam under the caliphate and the camp of
the West under the crusaders. The article ran under the title
"The Extinction of the Grayzone." The gray zone, the authors
explained, was the space inhabited by any Muslim who had not
joined the ranks of either ISIS or the crusaders. Throughout
the article, these Muslims were called "the grayish," "the hypocrites," and, for variety, "the grayish hypocrites."

As *Dabiq* made clear, ISIS wanted to eliminate the gray
zone of coexistence between religions and, through its terrorist attacks and the anti-Muslim backlash they caused, to create
a response that would force Muslims to choose sides: either
they would "adopt" the infidel religion of the crusaders or they
would "perform hijrah to the Islamic State." Although the
language that ISIS used in *Dabiq* may seem new, the message
was not. It had echoes of George W. Bush's famous proclama-

tion, after the terrorist attacks of September 11, that "either you are with us or you are with the terrorists." In addition, ISIS exploited the historical erasure of Muslim Americans by providing a counter-narrative of a simpler past, in which Muslim identity trumped all others—racial, ethnic, linguistic, and national. That past never existed.

These black-and-white views of the world leave no room for people like me. I'm Muslim, but I don't keep dietary laws or follow strict rituals. I speak my mind on justice and give to charity whenever I can, but I imagine that this would not be enough to save me were I to have the misfortune, through an accident of birth or migration, to live in a place ruled by ISIS, or another group like it. At the same time, I'm an American who doesn't support U.S. exceptionalism or military occupations. I vote in every election and serve on juries whenever I'm called upon, but these habits don't protect me from attacks by those who define patriotism as a blind support for the troops. The space I occupy is an intersection of identities—Arab, Muslim, and American.

Whose lives are gray? Mine, certainly. I was born in Morocco, spoke Arabic as a child, came to my love of literature through French, and now live in the U.S., where I write books and teach college classes in English. I have made my home in between these cultures, languages, and countries, and I have found it a glorious place to be. My friends come from different faiths or no faith, but each one makes my life richer. This gray life of mine is not unique. I share it with billions of people around the world. Most of the time, gray lives go unnoticed. People of different faiths live side by side in many countries, whether in the West or in the East, and no one finds this unusual or remarkable.

But when violence erupts—whether as a result of a terrorist

attack or a military invasion—battle lines are swiftly drawn, and gray lives become targets. At the height of its power, when ISIS was attacking Shia mosques in Iraq, Christian churches in Syria, or outdoor venues in Europe, it was tearing at the fabric of coexistence, causing each group to retreat into itself, flee for its safety, or fight them in a rising spiral of violence. In the United States, meanwhile, hate crimes against Muslims spike after every attack by ISIS, but rather than stigmatize the hate, politicians and pundits often stoke it with fiery rhetoric, further diminishing the zone of coexistence. Every time this gray zone recedes, tribalism and sectarianism gain ground.

Coexistence should not be a passive state. Having a sticker on one's car or a sign in one's yard is a beautiful gesture, and even a necessary one at times of division and hatred. But it is not enough. Coexistence, rather, should be the active practice of becoming familiar, whether through exposure to works of imagination or through personal interaction, with people who are different. In a multicultural nation, where citizens belong to distinct religious faiths, or no faith, that practice becomes an imperative. It is the glue that holds the community together and allows it to withstand external threats. The more citizens of different backgrounds know about one another, the better they are able to work together, form alliances on issues of common interest, and resist calls of division from merchants of war.

Political violence affects all of us in the same way: we experience sorrow and anger at the loss of life, we demand justice for the fallen, and we hear calls for retribution. For Muslims in America, however, there is an additional layer of grief as we ourselves become subjects of suspicion. We are called upon to condemn terrorism, but no matter how often or how loud or how clear the condemnations, the calls remain. We are asked to answer questions about terrorists, even in situations that have nothing to do with terrorism. We are, in other words, always on trial.

One morning, a few weeks after the reading I gave in Arizona, my daughter said to me, "I want to be president." It was a new ambition, which she voiced after watching a presidential debate between Donald Trump and Hillary Clinton, and our breakfast-table conversation veered toward the election. My daughter plays the violin and the guitar; she loves math and history; she's quick-witted and sharp-tongued; but above all, she's kind to others. "I'd vote for you," I told her. And then I looked away, because I didn't have the heart to tell her that half the people in this country—in her country—told pollsters that year that they wouldn't vote for a Muslim presidential candidate. American citizenship is still popularly perceived to be tied to religion, specifically Christianity. Being Muslim means being different, and therefore ineligible for the presidency.

My daughter still has the innocence and determination that are the natural attributes of the young, but what will happen when she comes of age and starts to realize that her citizenship, like mine, is often under question? I worry about her growing up in a place where many people, from the woman at the reading to candidates for the highest office in the land, cannot make a simple distinction between Islam and ISIS, between Muslim and terrorist. My daughter has never heard of the gray zone, though she has lived in it her entire life. Perhaps this writing is my attempt at keeping the world around all of us as gray as possible. It is a form of resistance, the only form of resistance I know.

Borders

The Border Patrol agent watched our Prius approach, then signaled for us to stop. Behind him stood several men in green uniforms, their hands resting on holsters and their eyes hidden behind sunglasses. Two German shepherds sat on the asphalt, panting and waiting in the humid heat. The agent put one hand on the driver's side window and, bending to our level, peered inside the car. "Are you a U.S. citizen?" he asked, pointing at each one of us. "Yes," said one of my friends, a visual artist from Iowa. "Yes," echoed the other, a poet from Connecticut. "Yes," I said from the back seat. The agent's gaze lingered on me for a moment, but then he stood up and waved us through the border.

Except this was not a border. This was on Interstate 10 in west Texas, somewhere between El Paso and Marfa. At the Sierra Blanca checkpoint, Border Patrol agents make arrests for drugs or weapons, share information with federal agencies, and turn undocumented immigrants over to Immigration and Customs Enforcement. My friends and I had been warned about this inspection point, and told to bring our passports with us *just in case*. In case of what remained unspecified, but as it happened the agent never asked for our papers. Perhaps the line of cars was too long that afternoon, or perhaps the presence of my two white friends served as a form of laissez-passer. Either way, a determination was made, and we were allowed to cross.

At the time, I thought that Sierra Blanca was an exception, the sort of curiosity you might come across in a book of strange but true facts about America. But later I discovered, on the website of Customs and Border Protection, that there are 136 checkpoints just like Sierra Blanca scattered throughout the continental United States. (The *Arizona Republic* estimated that, when temporary checkpoints are added to the count, the number may be as high as 200.) Sierra Blanca is perhaps the most notorious, because of its frequent celebrity arrests. Willie Nelson, Snoop Dogg, and Fiona Apple were all busted for marijuana possession when their tour buses passed through this station a few years ago. Other inspection points are rarely ever in the news. There is one near the Salton Sea, in California; one in Beecher Falls, Vermont; one in Buffalo, New York; and one in Lake Charles, Louisiana.

You might wonder, as I did when I found out about them, why the land of the free has so many checkpoints. It turns out that in 1952 the Justice Department gave Border Patrol agents the right to monitor all territory within twenty-five miles of a land border, which was then considered a reasonable distance for a search. A year later, that power was expanded to anywhere within a hundred miles of any external boundaries. (The decision to redefine *reasonable distance* as a hundred miles might have been made because of the long-standing tradition that witnesses under subpoena must attend a court hearing, trial, or deposition if they live within a hundred miles of where the subpoena was issued.) Border agents have the legal authority to set up checkpoints, question vehicle occupants about their citizenship status, and, if they have probable cause, whether through visual observation or the use of canines, search and seize anything deemed illegal. "Motorists may consent to a search," a fact sheet on CBP's website helpfully explains, "but they are not required to do so."

As a result of these Justice Department regulations, the borders of the continental United States are not just the clear lines that separate it from Canada and Mexico, but any place within a hundred miles of those perimeters, whether on dry land, ocean coast, or Great Lakes shore. This hundred-mile border strip encompasses almost entirely the states of Connecticut, Delaware, Florida, Hawaii, Maine, Massachusetts, Michigan, New Hampshire, New Jersey, New York, Rhode Island, and Vermont—along with the most populated parts of many others, including California and Illinois. In total, the hundred-mile-wide border zone is home to two-thirds of the nation's population.

This is such a staggering fact that it bears repeating: The vast majority of Americans, roughly 200 million, are effectively living in the border zone and could one day face checkpoints like the one I went through in Sierra Blanca, Texas. They can be asked about their citizenship status and if they don't carry a birth certificate or a passport with them and somehow fail to persuade the agent—because of how they look, act, or sound— they can be detained and referred to ICE. Each year, hundreds of U.S. citizens are wrongfully held in immigration jails, where they have to wait for months, and in a few cases years, to go before a federal judge. Although CBP inspection points like Sierra Blanca periodically attract media attention, their existence has never been seriously challenged. The checkpoints continue to operate, functioning like borders within borders.

. . .

Until that encounter with Border Patrol in Texas, my understanding of borders had been more rudimentary. To my mind, borders only marked the contours of nations, defining them by separating them from their neighbors. A border could be natural—an ocean, a river, a chain of mountains—or it could be artificial, splitting a homogeneous landscape or a unified people into two, as happened, for example, during the colonial era in Asia, Africa, and here in America. Often a border was highly literal, announcing itself in the shape of a concrete wall, a sand berm, a tall fence topped with barbed wire. But I hadn't considered that a border could also be expandable and movable, like the CBP checkpoints in the United States, which take the form of permanent as well as roving stations. I have since come to realize that, whatever form it takes, a border primarily conveys meaning about the Self and the Other.

A few hours before passing through Sierra Blanca, I was on an American Airlines flight from Los Angeles to El Paso. On my lap was the manuscript for a novel I had been working on, and which I hoped to finish while on an artist residency in Marfa. As the plane began its descent, I noticed from my window seat the border wall that separates El Paso from Ciudad Juárez, Mexico. On one side were gleaming towers, giant freeways, and sprawling parks; on the other, homes huddling together in the afternoon light, winding streets, and patches of dry grass. The two cities have a common language, a shared history, and a mixed culture that thrives on both sides of the Rio Grande—a natural border—but they were severed from each other when an eighteen-foot-tall fence was erected, cutting the landscape into two. After the excision, one city survived unharmed, while the other sank deeper into drug violence. The wall sent a message: on this side, you will find safety and prosperity, but over there lie danger and poverty.

The wall along the southern border is a relatively recent structure—it did not exist thirty years ago. The few chain-link fences between the U.S. and Mexico served mostly to prevent cattle from crossing the international line. In the fall of 1993, however, the Clinton administration authorized the Border Patrol to position hundreds of agents and vehicles along the border between El Paso and Ciudad Juárez. The purpose of this exercise, which was called Operation Hold the Line, was to see if a show of force might deter illegal crossings. Within weeks, the number of apprehensions at the El Paso station dropped and, although unlawful border crossings in nearby areas rose, the agent-vehicle blockade was considered a success. A year later, the Clinton administration launched Operation Gatekeeper. Under this new initiative, the government erected a twelve-foot-high steel fence at the border between San Diego and Tijuana, on a thirteen-mile stretch of land that leads to the Pacific Ocean. It was built using helicopter landing pads recycled from the Vietnam War, a pattern of reuse that the political scientist Victoria Hattam has called "imperial recycling." The number of illegal crossings in the San Diego area fell dramatically, an outcome that Janet Reno, then the attorney general, called "excellent." Once again, though, the flow of immigrants did not stop; it was merely redirected eastward, and, under the direction of smugglers, into deserts and mountains that were more treacherous to cross, with the result that a great number of immigrants died in the borderlands.

This was not perceived to be, in and of itself, a failure of policy. In 2006, George W. Bush signed into law the Secure Fence Act, which provided funding for seven hundred miles of fencing along the border between the United States and Mexico. "Unfortunately, the United States has not been in complete control of its borders for decades," he said at the signing ceremony, and the bill represented "an important step in our nation's efforts to secure our border and reform our immigration system." Over the next ten years, new portions of wall were built in California, Texas, Arizona, and New Mexico. The number of illegal crossings on the southern border declined steadily during that decade, a fact that Barack Obama cited as evidence of his own administration's seriousness about securing the border. At the same time, the number of immigrant deaths continued to rise. Accurate figures are difficult to come by, but the Border Patrol estimates that more than 7,500 immigrants have died in remote mountains and deserts since the first wall was erected.

Along with the building of these fences came an increased militarization of the border. Agents were given access to four-wheel-drive vehicles, portable radios, infrared night scopes, seismic sensors to detect traffic, and all kinds of other equipment typically used in defense operations. Between 1993 and 2017, the budget of the Border Patrol increased tenfold, rising from $363 million to $3.8 billion per fiscal year. I wonder sometimes if Americans feel ten times more secure now than they did in 1993. When they watch television at night, do retirees in Des Moines heave a sigh of relief and think how much safer they are today than in the bad old days? Do football fans who gather for a beer at a bar in Denver slap each other on the back and say, finally, we can do this in peace? Do parents pushing their strollers through a Whole Foods in Santa Barbara look at each other, amazed at how well protected they are, compared to the 1990s?

Although the southern border continued to materialize, the word "wall" was rarely used, either by elected officials or in the media. For a long time, the preferred terms were "fence," "barrier," "border defense," and "border-protection system." But all of these euphemisms were stripped away in 2015, when Donald Trump made one of his campaign slogans a simple three-word chant: *Build That Wall*. "When Mexico sends its people," he told a crowd of supporters at Trump Tower in New York City in 2015, "they're sending people that have lots of problems, and they're bringing those problems. They're bringing drugs. They're bringing crime. They're rapists." This was why, he said, he would build "a great, great wall," for which Mexico would pay. When Vicente Fox, former president of Mexico, declared that his nation had no intention of paying, Trump's response was "The wall just got 10 feet higher." The more the wall was challenged, the taller it became, as if boosting its height could make all rational debate about its morality, its efficacy, and its environmental impact disappear.

As time passed, however, Trump's promise began to shift. The wall was not needed along the entire 1,900-mile southern border, he said, because "we have natural barriers." For this reason, a 1,000-mile wall would suffice. And it didn't need to be a wall, either. It could be "a barrier," a "great steel barrier," a "very tough fence," a "slat fence," or "whatever you want to call it." As for the cost of construction, it would be "paid back by Mexico later," "reimbursed at a later date," or "paid for in a trade deal." In late 2018, in an attempt to force the U.S. government to pay for the wall, he furloughed 800,000 federal workers for more than three weeks, causing some of them to apply for loans to meet their mortgages or even to stand in line at food banks in Washington, D.C. Some people might look at the shifting rhetoric as evidence that Trump doesn't believe what he says, but in fact he has been remarkably consistent—even obsessive—about his goal: the creation of a physical marker between the United States and Mexico.

Whether the administration can manage the construction of vast sections of wall remains to be seen, but in the meantime, it is building the legal apparatus of a virtual wall. Speaking to Customs and Border Protection officers in Nogales, Arizona, in 2017, Jeff Sessions, then the attorney general, promised them "more tools in your fight against criminal aliens"—including charging immigrants who repeatedly cross into the U.S. illegally with felonies and, when possible, with document fraud and aggravated identity theft, which carry a mandatory prison time of two years. In his speech, Sessions consistently used the imagery of war. He described Nogales as "ground zero" in the fight to secure the border, a place where "ranchers work each day to make an honest living" while under threat from "criminal organizations that turn cities and suburbs into war zones, that rape and kill innocent civilians." Under the Trump administration, he said, the Justice Department was prepared to fight: "It is here, on this sliver of land, on this border, where we first take our stand." In Jeff Sessions's rhetoric, the southern border separates not just nationals from foreigners, rich from poor, or north from south, but also order from chaos, civilization from barbarians, and decent people from criminals. Location becomes character, with everything that this designation entails. A person is either American and an honest worker, or she is not American and is a criminal alien. The two categories are seen as inherent and inflexible. That, coincidentally, is the language of race.

One summer, I remember, while on a road trip to Arizona, my husband and I spent a night in Calexico, a small town at the border between California and Baja. The border post was less than a mile from our hotel, so we decided to cross into Mexicali early the next morning to watch a World Cup final match. Going through the pedestrian lane into Mexico was easy enough; once we passed the metal detector at Customs, no one even asked us for identification. We walked into Mexicali, where a tall cinder-block wall topped with barbed wire marked the line between the two countries, and found a restaurant where we could watch the game. But coming back to the United States afterward was a two-hour ordeal, which began with long lines in the oppressive heat. I had forgotten to bring a hat, and the sunlight gave me a migraine. Sweat ran down my back in a continuous stream. When we finally got inside, the border agent scanned our passports and peppered us with questions about our brief visit: Why did we watch the game on the other side? Which teams were playing? Whom did we root for? Why? At the other end of the room, a woman was pulled aside for additional questioning. Although I had done nothing wrong, I started to feel nervous, wondering whether the wrong word or the wrong facial expression might get us in trouble. Eventually, the agent got tired of grilling us and waved us through.

The northern border offered a sharp contrast. A few weeks later, when I drove from Seattle to Vancouver, I was immediately struck by the ease of the crossing. The passport-control building sat at the edge of a twenty-acre flowering garden—jointly owned by Washington State and British Columbia—which was called Peace Arch Park. Families with young children milled about, taking pictures by the gazebo or by the obelisk that marked the international line. Signs by the side of the road reminded travelers about the impending switch into the metric system: *50 kilometers per hour means 30 miles per hour*. In the distance, the sun glazed the Pacific Ocean. It was a bright day in August and the line of cars was long, but the experience was free of hassle.

This is particularly notable because the 5 freeway, which runs from Southern California to the Canadian border, constitutes one of the major corridors for drug trafficking. These days, drugs like fentanyl and ecstasy flow into the U.S. from Canada, just as OxyContin did in the 2000s or heroin in the 1980s. And the traffic isn't restricted to the 5 freeway, either. Because the northern border is longer than the southern border (5,500 miles compared to 1,900 miles), it provides many more opportunities for crossing in remote areas. Yet the president never referred to Canadians as criminals or drug dealers, nor did the attorney general make special visits to Border Patrol agents in Blaine, Washington, to deliver speeches about the dichotomy between good and evil.

While the U.S. and Canada have agreements that allow their citizens to visit without visas, undocumented immigration still happens. In this particular form of migration, however, the unlawful part comes after the lawful part. According to a 2016 report by the Department of Homeland Security that tracked air and sea arrivals, Canada has the most estimated visa overstays (about 93,000) in the United States, which is twice as many as Mexico (42,000), and five times as many as Colombia (16,000). But U.S. politicians don't accuse Canadians of "stealing" jobs, as they so regularly do with Central and South Americans, nor is the specter of rape and crime ever raised. No wall has ever been suggested for the border with Canada. It's clear that the southern border conveys something about America's sense of itself that the northern border doesn't, which makes the wall, the great steel barrier, the tough fence, the slat fence, or whatever you want to call it, a racialized structure.

. . .

I had my first border experience without having to leave my country. In 1977, when I was still a child, my parents packed my siblings and me in our old Renault and took us on the first of many road trips to the north of Morocco. We swam in the warm waters off Asilah's beaches, ate fried sardines at a lunch counter in Larache, and stayed a few days in Tetuan, a beautiful town nestled in the Rif mountains. From there we drove to Melilla, on the Mediterranean Sea. The city of Melilla is an anomaly: it is politically a part of Spain, but it is located in Morocco, a hold-over from medieval Spanish incursions on the African coast. It was only after we arrived at the border post—in those days, a tiny, cinder-block building—that it dawned on my parents that my ten-month-old brother had not been added to either of their passports. He had no papers. "Should we turn back?" my mother asked.

"We'd lose the whole day," my father said. "Let's just give it a try."

We waited in the long line of idling cars. My sister and I played with our dolls in the back seat, I remember, while the Bee Gees blared from the radio. When our turn finally came, the Spanish border guard checked our passports, then asked about my little brother's. My father explained he'd been so busy since the baby was born, he hadn't had a chance to get him one. "But we're only staying the day," he said.

"One day?" the guard asked. "All right." And he lifted the barrier.

We drove along Melilla's streets toward downtown, where many of the shops were closing. *Why was that*, I wondered aloud. Melilla is on Spanish time, my father explained, and though it was only 11:30 a.m. on our side of the border, over here it was already 1:30 p.m. Time for afternoon siesta. To my child's mind, it seemed as though we had crossed through a magical gate that had made time speed up. Surely, other wonders awaited us. But while more people spoke Spanish and there were more churches on this side, the landscape looked much the same as on our side. The streets were paved with cobblestones, the city walls were ocher-colored, and palm trees swayed in the wind. If the border held any meaning for me, it was only that it separated Spaniards from Moroccans, the way the fence in our yard separated us from the family next door.

Nowadays, though, Melilla is a different place. The city is surrounded by a twelve-foot-wide ditch, a wall topped with blades, and three metal fences, two of which are twenty feet high. The border perimeter is surveilled by cameras, protected by motion-activated alarms, and patrolled by a multitude of Spanish guards equipped with the latest technologies, including night-vision goggles. The area looks like an obstacle course for mythical giants. In the mountainous areas that surround the city, makeshift camps house West African immigrants who spent months traveling north to Morocco, hoping to cross into Europe. The wall in Melilla no longer delineates a national border. Instead, it has come to signify something deeper: it segregates Spaniards from Moroccans, Europeans from Africans, Christians from Muslims, and white people from brown or black people. The wall's message is clear and blunt. Keep out.

The transformation of the small cinder-block building in Melilla into a modern fortress happened slowly, day by day. In the 1970s, when my family took that day trip through the city, there were no visa requirements for Moroccans to enter Spain, nor for Spaniards to enter Morocco. Seasonal workers from Morocco could come to work on the farms and return home for the rest of the year. Spaniards, too, came to Morocco seeking economic opportunity or fleeing political persecution. I remember, for instance, that the family physician who gave me all my vaccines was a Spanish dissident who had settled in Rabat, my hometown.

After the death of Francisco Franco in 1975, Spain slowly transitioned from dictatorship to democracy, whereas Morocco remained stuck in "democratization," a process of never-ending reforms that firmly maintained power in the hands of the king. Then, in 1986, Spain joined the European Union and grew its economy, while Morocco began a period of economic decline, further exacerbated by World Bank debt-restructuring programs that resulted in severe cuts to social and educational services. The increasing disparities between the two countries meant that the flow of workers from the southern side of the border grew exponentially. In response, Spain imposed visa restrictions on Moroccans in 1991. These constraints did not stop the migratory flow, but split it into two—a legal route and an illegal route.

Moroccans who were desperate to find work or to join family members in Europe began to cross into Spain illegally, either at the land border with Ceuta and Melilla, or by crossing the Mediterranean Sea on lifeboats. Over the next twenty years, immigrants and asylum-seekers started to come from many other parts of Africa—Nigeria, Senegal, Mali, Sierra Leone, and elsewhere—to Morocco, where they, too, tried their luck at the border. The European Union responded to this economic and humanitarian crisis by imposing even tougher immigration policies, and giving massive funds to both Spain and Morocco to police their borders, turning the two neighboring countries into the policemen of their respective continents, reporting to the sergeants in Brussels. This was how Melilla became a modern fortress, complete with a six-foot-deep moat and armed guards watching from towers.

It is a rule of global migration that the tougher the policies, the more resourceful the immigrants. After all, people who are fleeing crushing poverty, civil war, or political persecution; who've spent months traveling on roads, in boats, or across the Sahara; and who've already paid thousands of dollars to smugglers are unlikely to change their minds because policy-makers in distant capitals suddenly rewrote this or that regulation. When higher fences were erected around Melilla, people used ladders to climb over them. When more guards were posted, people scaled the fence en masse, making it harder for the guards to stop all of them at once. When anti-climb mesh was installed on the fence, people foiled it by attaching hooks and screws to their shoes. Each obstacle fuels the immigrants' ingenuity. Periodically, hundreds of them try to storm Melilla's triple fences together, a tactic that is meant to overwhelm the guards. The crossing is demanding and dangerous, and most of the immigrants are immediately repelled. But a few make it through each time. Occasionally, some get stuck at the top of the last fence, a place of physical ambiguity and legal uncertainty. On one side, they see Europe. On the other, Africa. If they climb down, they will be arrested by border agents on one side or the other. And so, for a while, they wait, as if hoping for a miracle—a distraction, perhaps, which might make it possible for them to complete the crossing and reach the town itself. In the end, these few stragglers usually come down and return to their makeshift camps, waiting for another chance to try.

Spain erected the fences at Melilla ostensibly to boost its security, but in many ways the walls have increased violence at the border. Because Melilla is a tax-free city and personal luggage can be brought duty-free into Morocco, a lucrative business has emerged: wholesalers hire poor Moroccan women to carry electronics and other consumer goods from one side of the border to the other. Any day of the week, these women, some of whom are in their fifties and sixties, can be seen at the Barrio Chino pedestrian crossing, bent under as much as 150 pounds of merchandise. Sometimes the women collapse under their loads. Meanwhile, sub-Saharan women who have traveled thousands of miles north to reach this border face challenges of their own. In the makeshift camps where they live as they wait to cross, these women and girls are vulnerable to attacks, including assault and rape. In addition to all this, Moroccan police also frequently raid the camps, destroy the tents, and disperse the sub-Saharan immigrants to other parts of the country to prevent them from gathering in large enough groups to scale the fences together. "If you come here every day," a border guard told the BBC in 2013, "you begin to think that what you see is normal. But it isn't normal."

There was a time, and it was not so long ago, when Americans viewed erecting walls as the work of tyrants and autocrats. On his visit to China in 1972, Richard Nixon used his stop at the Great Wall to stress that "one of the results of our trip, we hope, may be that the walls that are erected, whether physical walls like this or whether they are other walls, ideology and philosophy, will not divide the people of the world." Fifteen years later, in June 1987, Ronald Reagan gave a speech on East-West relations at the Brandenburg Gate. "We come to Berlin," he said, "because it's our duty to speak, in this place, of freedom." Addressing the spectators, he decried the "vast system of barriers," both concrete and virtual, that contributed to "the brutal division" of Europe. The speech had been preceded by a flurry of media attention as well as popular protests, and I remember watching coverage of it on television in Morocco. I remember especially the dramatic moment when Reagan declared, "Mr. Gorbachev, tear down this wall."

Two years later, the German people tore down the wall themselves, and danced on its ruins. The night of November 9 was supposed to herald the start of a new era, and yet in the three decades that followed, new walls have been built—each designed to separate people along a new line, whether ethnic, national, or religious. Nowadays the West is constructing its own version of the Iron Curtain, one based not on political ideology, but on the identity of undesirable asylum-seekers or immigrants. What will future historians call it, this global network of walls? Will it get an Orwellian name, like Freedom Wall? Or will it end up with a more descriptive title, like the Wall of Segregation?

Parts of this wall have already been erected. In 2015, at the height of the Syrian refugee crisis, Hungary built a hundred-mile-long barrier along its border with Serbia and Croatia, forcing the flow of asylum-seekers to shift to its neighbors. In 2016, the French and British governments built a wall in the seaside town of Calais to separate the refugee camp there, which housed Iraqi Kurds and Eastern African migrants, from the highway leading to the Channel. That same year, Austria built a wall along its border with Slovenia. And Turkey is currently building a 515-mile-long wall to separate itself from Syria. In each case, the stated goal is to protect the Self from various Others: those who might take away natives' jobs; might constitute a drain on public resources; might bring with them strange customs; might not assimilate into the local culture; might look, sound, or worship differently; might even be, and this is the accusation that stifles nearly all discussion, *terrorists*. Whatever role the government on one side of the wall might have played in causing masses of people to show up on the other side is rarely the subject of serious debate.

I have seen a few of the walls myself. In Bethlehem some years ago, I walked along the concrete wall that cuts through Palestinian territories like a scar. The wall is almost completely covered with graffiti—slogans of resistance, mostly, as well as messages from the occupied territories. One of them said "Happy Christmas from Bethlehem." There, in the birthplace of a man who preached about loving your neighbor as you love yourself, I stood in line at a checkpoint, walked through a narrow metal cage, and waited to be searched by Israeli guards with semi-automatic weapons casually slung across their shoulders. I was fortunate: I could go through a special lane for visitors. I didn't have to be there at three in the morning, when hundreds of Palestinian workers are herded through this narrow gate so they can get to their jobs inside Israel, the passageway leading to it so crowded that older people faint. "We are human beings," an elderly man named Abu Ashraf told Israel's Channel One. "What's the difference between us and animals who go through a checkpoint like this?"

In Ramallah, I went hiking with a dozen people, most of them poets and writers who, like me, were guests of a local literary festival. The hills were terraced with olive trees and the earth, when you grabbed a fistful of it, was red and warm. The presence of the wall around the town turned even the enjoyment of nature into a dangerous act. We met a Palestinian who told us he was an avid hiker, although he had to be extremely careful when he was out on the hills, because if he mistakenly stepped on an Israeli settlement he might be fired at or set upon with dogs. In Hebron, I walked down Shuhada Street, where the doors of Palestinian homes and businesses were welded shut by the Israeli army in 1994. The men, women, and children who lived on that street could only enter from the back of the buildings, like intruders into their own homes.

Dehumanization is a feature of border walls. In Melilla, the women who carry duty-free bales from Spain to Morocco are called "porteadoras," meaning, strictly speaking, carriers, but in the Spanish press, they are sometimes referred to as "mujeres mulas," or women mules. On a visit to Calais in 2015, David Cameron, then the British prime minister, reassured his compatriots that they were safe despite the "swarm of people" coming from across the Mediterranean. The Calais camp has now been dismantled, but it was once known as "the Jungle." In the United States, people who cross the border and claim asylum are placed in the notorious "hieleras" or iceboxes, so called because of how cold the rooms are and because they are located in ICE facilities. Those who cross the border unlawfully and are detained by border agents are held in CBP facilities, where they are placed in cages known as "perreras," or dog kennels. When Donald Trump shut down the federal government in December 2018 to force Congress to fund his border wall, one of his sons took to social media to ask "You know why you can enjoy a day at the zoo? Because walls work." The fact that the president's son had likened immigrants to animals barely made a blip, so desensitized had most Americans become to the dehumanizing rhetoric on migration. I thought about the border guard in Melilla: *If you come here every day, you begin to think that this is normal. But it isn't normal.*

After our encounter with Border Patrol at Sierra Blanca, my friends and I drove another hundred miles to our destination.

Marfa was in many ways an ideal place for a novelist in the final stages of manuscript revision. The town was small—about three thousand people—and quiet. Owing to its history with the artist Donald Judd, it had a number of art installations, galleries, and museums, but it had few other distractions: no movie theater, no concert venue, not even a department store. The most exciting social event in the six weeks I spent there was a high school football game between the Marfa Shorthorns and the Fort Hancock Mustangs. Although I had a car, I left it in the garage and walked everywhere. One afternoon, a few days after I arrived, I was having a drink in the courtyard of the El Paisano, dreamily thinking about James Dean and Elizabeth Taylor, who'd stayed at this hotel during the filming of *Giant*, when I noticed a group of Border Patrol agents at a table nearby. "Is something the matter?" I asked the server. "Not at all," he replied. "They come in here all the time."

It turned out there was *another* Border Patrol checkpoint, this one south of Marfa. I started to notice the agents' white trucks when I went to the post office or the bookstore or the farmers' market. I noticed, too, the highway patrol's cruisers, the state troopers' cars, and the Marfa police SUVs that drove along San Antonio Street at all hours. For such a small town, Marfa seemed to have a large police presence. What would it be like to live in a place like this, I wondered. More broadly, how did residents of border towns manage their inevitable daily interactions with agents of the state?

The questions were pertinent to my interest in citizenship. After all, the border is an in-between space, where laws that seem settled elsewhere may not always apply. At points of entry into the United States, for example, no traveler—whether tourist, refugee, immigrant, or citizen—is fully protected by the Fourth Amendment, which safeguards against unreasonable searches and seizures. Customs and Border Protection officers have the power to search luggage as well as phones, tablets, and laptops. They can ask for online browsing histories and passwords to social-media accounts. A poorly phrased joke on Twitter, a compromising picture on a private Instagram account, a Facebook argument with a crazy uncle—all these could be readable by CBP officers and, if deemed relevant, turned over to law enforcement.

However, at the checkpoints it operates inside the country, Border Patrol is bound by the Fourth Amendment, which theoretically protects everyone, regardless of race or ethnicity. Still, agents wield a lot of discretionary power: they can decide whom to let go and whom to pull aside, question, and send to secondary inspection. This power was tested in a landmark case known as *Martinez-Fuerte*. In the summer of 1974, Amado Martinez-Fuerte, a lawful immigrant, was stopped at the San Clemente checkpoint, sixty miles south of Los Angeles, and asked about his immigration status. He produced his green card, but his passengers, both of them women, admitted to being in the country illegally. Martinez-Fuerte was subsequently charged with "illegally transporting aliens." His lawyer filed a motion to suppress, based on the fact that the evidence was collected without probable cause—in other words, the agents had no valid reason to pull Martinez-Fuerte's vehicle aside. The case went to appeal, along with other similar cases, and, in 1976, the Supreme Court ruled that Border Patrol agents do have the narrow authority to ask about immigration status at permanent checkpoints (but not at roving checkpoints) and to visually inspect vehicles. Given the high volume of traffic at the southern border, the Court further decided, agents can use "Mexican ancestry" as a criterion for deciding whom to pull aside.

In establishing this precedent, the Supreme Court essentially classified Americans of Mexican ancestry—as well as those who appear to be of Mexican ancestry—as conditional citizens. They are more likely to undergo inspections, face seizures, or end up in immigration detention, where they have to wait to go before a federal judge to prove their citizenship. Justice William Brennan, who dissented from the ruling in *Martinez-Fuerte*, foresaw that it would lead to racial profiling: "Every American citizen of Mexican ancestry and every Mexican alien lawfully in this country must know after today's decision that he travels the fixed checkpoint highways at the risk of being subjected not only to a stop, but also to detention and interrogation, both prolonged and to an extent far more than for non-Mexican appearing motorists." Border Patrol checkpoints have a tangible impact on the towns in which they operate, an impact felt most acutely by Latinx residents. Commuting to work or going to the grocery store can mean having to cross a checkpoint, with all the discretionary power—and potential for abuse—that this involves.

A few years ago, the residents of Arivaca, a small town in southern Arizona, became so frustrated with the racial profiling that they set up a watch group to monitor their local Border Patrol checkpoint. As the *Arizona Daily Star* reported, residents recorded data for 2,379 vehicle stops and turned them over to an independent statistician. The results showed that Latinx motorists were much more likely to be asked to show identification or to be pulled for secondary inspection. Of the daily hassle by agents, Carlota Wray, a Mexican-American woman who had to go through the checkpoint each time she took her grandchildren to school, said, "It must be my color. I'm a Mexican."

While the Border Patrol provides data on illegal drugs and

unregistered firearms it seizes every year, it does not release statistics on vehicle stops or on the race and ethnicity of travelers it requires to prove citizenship. Over the years, the discretionary power granted by the Supreme Court in *Martinez-Fuerte* has led to a form of policing reserved specifically for people of Mexican ancestry, and which can be observed far from the southern border. In May 2018, two American citizens, Ana Suda and Martha Hernandez, were detained by a Border Patrol agent in Havre, Montana, after he heard them speak Spanish in a grocery store. During their interrogation, the agent's supervisor arrived, and Suda asked him if they would have been stopped if they had been speaking French. "No, we don't do that," the supervisor said, according to the suit filed by the ACLU on the women's behalf. In a statement, Suda said that the incident had made her young daughter afraid to speak Spanish.

Even those who do not cross borders and checkpoints can be affected by them; mere proximity will suffice. A couple of years ago, the *Washington Post* reported that hundreds of Americans born in the Rio Grande valley in south Texas had been denied passports by the State Department—including a man who was a Border Patrol officer himself. (Denials of passports began during the Bush administration and continued into the Obama and Trump administrations.) These citizens had birth certificates that listed their attending physician as a midwife, a common tradition among communities in the rural South, and the government claimed that, because of a few fraudulent cases in the past, such birth certificates could not be accepted as proof of identification. (There have been no similar reports of passport denials for people born at home in places far from the border, like Brooklyn or Santa Monica.) As a result, Americans born under the care of a midwife in border towns like Brownsville, Texas, could, at any time, have their passport applications denied. This, too, is an effect of the border: it puts into question the citizenship of Americans closest to it.

As I got to the end of my residency in Marfa, my walks around the town became longer, leading me to open fields where grass grew tall and thick. Watching the Sandhill cranes traveling across the sky in flocks, it occurred to me that human beings, too, are a migratory species. When their natural habitat no longer affords them safety, stability, or opportunity, they leave home and find shelter somewhere new. After all, the story of humanity is fundamentally a story of migration: Adam was forced out of Eden, Moses led his people out of Egypt, Muhammad made the hegira to Mecca. This is why efforts to stop the movement of people strike me as futile, like trying to stop birds from flying south for the winter.

Our species has now reached a turning point. Scientists predict that, unless we take radical and sustained action, the earth will warm by as much as two degrees Celsius over the next decade. The likelihood of extreme weather events has increased dramatically all around the world. Even the calendar has begun to reflect the change, with news reports routinely covering "hurricane season" or "wildfire season." In California, where I live, many people have been advised by local governments to keep, alongside their earthquake kits, wildfire kits: fire extinguisher, battery-powered radio, water, medications. But the kits don't say where we are supposed to go if a fire breaks out. Migration is not just an economic or political issue; increasingly, it is also a climate issue.

For now, most Americans are still safe from displacement. They might hear of war in the Middle East or violence in South America, yet feel removed from their government's responsibility in igniting the conflict. They might see images of drought and flooding in Africa and Asia, yet refuse to confront the consequences of unfettered industrialization and capitalistic growth. Being on the "right" side of a wall gives the illusion of security. When a climate disaster strikes, however, internal migration will be the inevitable result. What, then, will be the use of the border wall or, for that matter, border checkpoints?

The border is a place of cultural contact, hybrid identity, and political complexity. Erecting a concrete fence over this gray space indicates a yearning for simplicity, which makes border walls literal expressions of our worst fears. Terrorists, rapists, drug dealers, and various "bad hombres" are all said to come from somewhere else. Drawing clear, concrete boundaries will keep *us* safe from *them*. But wherever they have been built, border walls have been monuments of failure: they've put migration routes in the hands of traffickers, caused thousands of unnecessary deaths, dehumanized immigrants, discriminated against citizens of particular ancestries, and generally segregated people along ethnic, racial, or religious lines. As governments around the world continue to erect more border walls, this is another message worth apprehending: walls do not simply keep others out; they also keep us in.

Assimilation

"The problem is," my seatmate said, "they don't assimilate." We were 30,000 feet in the air, an hour from our destination in Reno, and I was beginning to regret the turn our conversation had taken. It had started out as small talk, while we waited for the flight's beverage service. He told me he owned a butcher shop in Gardena, about fifteen miles south of Los Angeles, but was contemplating retirement. I knew the area well, having lived nearby when I was in graduate school, though I hadn't been there in years. "Oh, it's changed a lot," he told me. "We have all those Koreans now." Ordinarily, my instinct would have been to return to the novel I was reading, but this was just two months after the election of Donald Trump on a viciously anti-immigrant platform, and I was still trying to parse for myself what was happening in the country. I asked my seatmate what he meant. "They have their own schools," he said. "They send their kids there on Sundays so they can learn Korean."

The word *assimilate* rolls off the tongue so inoffensively it's hard to imagine it used as a cudgel. And yet that is how it appears in conversation: used in discussions about immigrants, it's more often than not a complaint or an accusation. Newcomers to America are expected, over an unspecified period of time, to become more like other Americans, a process meta-

phorically described as a melting pot: each pure metal is supposed to melt into the existing alloy. The image evokes a nation
that becomes stronger as new immigrants join it, an ideal that
is frequently brought up in moments of patriotic fervor, like
the World Series or the Olympic Games. But the population
of the United States is heterogeneous—as it has been since its
founding—and the criteria by which a person is judged to fit
into such a diverse nation remain unclear, at least to me. Over
the years, I've noticed that, for some Americans, the assimilation of immigrants is based on pragmatic considerations, like
civic engagement or familiarity with the country's history or
culture. For others, however, assimilation runs much deeper
and involves relinquishing all ties to the old country. It seemed
to aggrieve my seatmate on that plane, for example, that there
were families in Gardena who wanted their children to speak
the language of their ancestors.

These contradictory expectations reflect the historical relationship between the United States and its immigrants. On
the one hand, immigration has long been viewed as an important asset to the nation. Newcomers represented an estimated
5 percent of population growth in 1790, when the first census
was collected, but as the government displaced indigenous
people and expanded its territory westward, that percentage
grew to a substantial 32 percent. By 1850, one out of every
three new Americans was an immigrant. In 1863, Abraham
Lincoln called immigration a "source of national wealth and
strength" and asked Congress to provide assistance to foreign
nationals who wanted to resettle here. Harry Truman credited
immigrants with making the country strong during the Second World War: "One of the reasons we lead the free world
today is that we are a nation of immigrants." Between 1903
and 1954, people arriving at Ellis Island were greeted by a cop-

per statue whose pedestal bore the words "Give me your tired, your poor, your huddled masses yearning to breathe free." One of America's most cherished myths is the idea that, no matter where you come from or what your background is, if you work hard, you can be successful here. Lin-Manuel Miranda's *Hamilton*, one of the most critically acclaimed and commercially successful Broadway shows in history, popularized the slogan "Immigrants, we get the job done."

On the other hand, the Founders did not imagine the United States as a multicultural haven; rather, they envisioned a society in which the highest privileges of citizenship were reserved for propertied white men and where immigration served their political and economic interests. In his *Notes on the State of Virginia*, Thomas Jefferson expressed skepticism that immigrants drawn from European monarchies would be able to assimilate to the newly founded nation: "They will bring with them the principles of the governments they leave, imbibed in their early youth; or, if able to throw them off, it will be in exchange for an unbounded licentiousness, passing, as is usual, from one extreme to another. . . . They will infuse into [legislation] their spirit, warp and bias its direction, and render it a heterogeneous, incoherent, distracted mass." These fears meant that newcomers to the U.S. were often met with deep suspicion or outright rejection. In 1890, for example, the *New York Times* cautioned that, while "the red and the black assimilate" in New York, "the yellow man" was different because he "was content to remain what he is." Chinese immigrants could not integrate, the paper told its readers, because they "refuse to surrender their own dress, their own art, their own cumbrous writing, their singularly flat religion." That same year, in one of the largest mass lynching in U.S. history, eleven Italians were murdered in New Orleans after some of them were acquitted in the killing of the local police chief, an event that led to another editorial in the *Times*, this time warning about "the descendants of bandits and assassins, who have transported to this country the lawless passions . . . of their native country." Cartoons of the era frequently depicted Irish refugees as drunken apes, unsuitable for civilized company.

Racist perceptions of newcomers were matched by legal restrictions on immigration. Laws curbing Asian immigration began with prohibitions on Chinese women in 1875 and expanded over the next few decades to include Chinese laborers, Japanese nationals, and eventually all Asians. The Johnson-Reed Act of 1924, which banned immigrants from Asian countries, also established national-origin quotas to drastically limit the arrival of nonwhite immigrants as well as those who were deemed insufficiently white—eastern and southern Europeans, for example. By 1930, a Texas congressman named John C. Box made the case to his colleagues on the House Immigration and Naturalization Committee that Mexicans, too, needed to be excluded from immigration because their culture had long tolerated miscegenation and therefore they would promote "a distressing process of mongrelization." He was ultimately unsuccessful, but the Census Bureau created a separate category that year for "Mexican." (The category was removed ten years later.) At different times in its history, the United States barred or curtailed the arrival of Asians, Italians, Irish, Jews, and Muslims. Each time, poor assimilation into white Protestant society was used as the reason for curbing immigration.

The pendulum continues to swing between hope and fear. Year after year, multiculturalists hail immigration as the lifeblood of this nation, while nativists portray immigrants as the gravest threat to it. In November 1990, George H. W. Bush signed into law an immigration bill that dramatically increased the total number of immigrant visas and diversified the categories under which immigrants could apply, a piece of legislation that, he said, "recognizes the fundamental importance and historic contributions of immigrants to our country." But this sweeping legislation led to an almost immediate backlash from his own party. The first time I saw Pat Buchanan on television, he was announcing his 1992 presidential campaign from a stage in New Hampshire, with the pledge that he would "put the needs of Americans first." He told his supporters that "our Judeo-Christian values are going to be preserved" and promised that "our Western heritage is going to be handed down to future generations and not dumped into some landfill called multiculturalism." At the time, Buchanan's position was viewed as being on the fringe of his party, but since then the national conversation has moved incrementally rightward. In the most recent presidential campaign, for example, Donald Trump warned that "not everyone who seeks to join our country will be able to successfully assimilate."

Growing up in Morocco, I never heard about assimilation except on TV5, the French satellite network we occasionally watched for news not covered by our local channels. Nearly every week, TV5 carried reports on the increasing anxiety in Paris about *les immigrés* from North Africa and their presumed inability to integrate successfully into modern society. As it happened, I knew several immigrants, most of them French teachers in the schools, both private and public, that I attended in Rabat. Perhaps my favorite was my sixth-grade French teacher, Olga Brun. I loved her first name—so reminiscent of the big Russian novels that I had just started reading—as well as her theatrics in the classroom. When we worked on our conjugations, Madame Brun would sit at her desk, put a Gauloise in her cigarette holder, and smoke while we made our way through *Bescherelle*. She was very tall, tanned in a 1980s-beach-resort kind of way, and wore her black hair in a braid that reached halfway down her back. At the end of the school year, I won an award and Madame Brun gave me a gift that I still have on my bookshelves in Los Angeles: a copy of Marcel Pagnol's novel *Le Chateau de ma mère*. On the first page, she wrote: "Thank you for a wonderful year spent together. Don't correct Lili's misspellings, as you mischievously corrected my omissions on the blackboard!" (Reader, I had no idea.)

Madame Brun had lived in Morocco for many years— I didn't know how old she was, but to my eleven-year-old self, she seemed to be fifty, which is to say *ancient*. Her teaching job was made possible by a cooperation agreement between France and Morocco, which was instituted after independence, when Morocco needed to hire thousands of educators at once. These were stable, well-paying positions, and many teachers stayed on for decades. Madame Brun had previously taught in Togo before moving to Morocco. She didn't speak a word of Arabic. If my parents wanted to discuss my schoolwork, they had to communicate with Madame Brun in French. What stands out to me now is that no one thought this odd, and no one questioned it.

Madame Brun wasn't alone. Over my years of K–12 schooling, I must have had ten or fifteen French teachers in subjects as varied as math, biology, and physics. They made no detectable effort to learn our language. They didn't change their mode of dress to better fit into our society, they weren't asked to learn the history of our country. None of them were challenged about this, or hassled by the police and told to show their identity papers. The reason is clear: assimilation is primarily about power.

My French teachers may have been immigrants, but their relationship to their host country replicated a dynamic that had started when Sultan Abdelhafid signed the Treaty of Fes in 1912. Morocco became a French colony and, although it regained its independence four decades later, the balance of power remained tilted to one side. I never once heard the king or any member of parliament express outrage that French immigrants eat pork, drink wine, or have extramarital sex, in contradiction of local norms, yet I heard dozens of French politicians complain about, as Jacques Chirac put it in 1991, "an overdose" of immigrants who refuse to assimilate. As mayor of Paris, Chirac famously lamented that French workers had to endure "the noise and the smell" of the immigrant family next door, "with a father, three or four wives, twenty kids, taking in 50,000 Francs in welfare payments without working." Four years later, he became president. (After his retirement, Chirac spent his holidays in Marrakesh and Taroudant, where, presumably, "the noise and the smell" didn't bother him any longer.)

Demands for assimilation are not all that different in the United States. The settlers didn't assimilate to indigenous tribes, learn their languages, and adapt to their cultural customs. It was the Natives who were assimilated, coercively and violently, into the settlers' culture. In the late eighteenth century, the U.S. government embarked on periodic and extensive efforts to "civilize" Indians by teaching them the values of Christianity, private property, and urban living. The Bureau of Indian Affairs separated indigenous children from their parents and placed them in off-reservation boarding schools, where they were forbidden to keep their birth names, speak their mother tongues, practice their ancestral faiths, or wear their hair in Native styles. These institutions were modeled after the Carlisle Indian Industrial School, founded by an army officer by the name of Richard Henry Pratt, who explained his philosophy in a speech delivered at the National Conference of Charities and Corrections in 1892: "A great general has said that the only good Indian is a dead one, and that high sanction of his destruction has been an enormous factor in promoting Indian massacres. In a sense, I agree with the sentiment, but only in this: that all the Indian there is in the race should be dead. Kill the Indian in him, and save the man." In this mindset, the only way for an indigenous person to achieve full humanity and fellowship with other Americans was to relinquish his or her heritage entirely. The consequences of forced assimilation are still being felt centuries later. Many Native names have been lost, and much of indigenous history has been erased or devalued, not least in the textbooks to which children are exposed in school. Of the 300 distinct languages that were spoken in America prior to contact with European settlers, there remain today only 154. The surviving languages often have few speakers; seven of them are down to just one speaker each. With language loss comes the loss of precious cultural heritage, from foundational stories to ancestral practices.

Enslaved people who were brought to the United States between 1619 and 1860 were also acculturated in a variety of ways: they were given new names, converted to Christianity, and forced to speak the masters' language. But that is where the similarities with the forced assimilation of indigenous people end. The same government that wanted to conform indigenous people to white society worked hard to ensure that enslaved people could not be assimilated. In southern states, a slew of laws made it illegal for whites to teach slaves or freedmen how to read, with punishment ranging from fines to flogging and imprisonment. After the Haitian revolution of 1804, in which Toussaint Louverture—a literate man—led his people to freedom, plantation owners feared that literacy would lead to rebellion. If there was any instruction, it was restricted to religion and circumscribed in ways that did not threaten the existing social and political order. A special edition of the Bible, printed in 1807 for use by plantation owners to preach to their slaves, omitted mention of the Israelites' flight from slavery in Egypt as well as other references to freedom. The book—*Parts of the Holy Bible, Selected for the Use of Negro Slaves in the British West India Islands*—had only 232 verses, compared with 1,189 for a standard Protestant Bible. Assimilation of the races was never the objective of a system that was designed to maintain one race in absolute and hereditary servitude to another. Even after the Emancipation Proclamation, Jim Crow laws ensured that black people remained separate from white people in every sphere of public life.

But the issue of assimilation came up during the civil rights movement, when the prospect of different races living side by side could no longer be avoided. Movement leaders had different opinions on this issue, but they all used new language: integration. Integration was different from assimilation, in that it envisioned Americans of all backgrounds interacting with one another as equals while retaining their cultural specificity. In this view, the proper metaphor for the country was not a melting pot, but a salad bowl. Martin Luther King's strategy for achieving civic equality and economic opportunity was through integration of black people. The Montgomery bus boycott and the Birmingham campaign, for example, were efforts at desegregating public and work spaces that the white hegemony controlled. By contrast, Malcolm X initially rejected integration because he did not believe it could guarantee freedom from physical violence or systemic oppression. In a debate with Bayard Rustin at Howard University in 1962, Malcolm declared flatly that "our only hope is not integration with a doomed society, but complete separation from a doomed society." Only later, toward the end of his life, did he come to see that voting and civic participation were the way forward in the struggle for equality.

All other groups who came to America did so willingly, either in search of freedom or opportunity. In the sixteenth century, Spanish conquistadors landed in Florida, sailed around the Gulf, and marched into the Southwest with indigenous Mexicans. In the seventeenth century, English, Dutch, and Swedish immigrants arrived, settling in New England, New York, and Delaware. Over the next three centuries, they were followed by Irish, Chinese, Japanese, Italian, Jewish, Middle Eastern, and South Asian immigrants, among many others. Each new group of immigrants was viewed with suspicion and blamed for a variety of problems: the Italians were said to bring crime, the Irish to enjoy debauchery, the Mexicans to steal jobs, and the Japanese to engage in sedition.

As the accusations spread, laws generally followed. Starting in 1850, several measures were passed to prevent Chinese people from obtaining citizenship, owning property, voting, serving on juries, testifying in court, attending white schools, or living in white neighborhoods. In the 1930s, the U.S. government repatriated as many as two million Mexicans, half of whom were U.S. citizens, under the pretext that they were to blame for the economic downturn. Los Angeles County, which had a large Mexican-American community, was the site of the largest and most violent wave of repatriation, with police officers rounding up people of Mexican heritage in their neighborhoods and sending them off with a one-way bus ticket south of the border. And in 1942, Franklin D. Roosevelt ordered the removal and internment of Japanese and Japanese-Americans in concentration camps, citing protection against war espionage and sabotage.

In spite of these restrictions, members of these communities managed to build lives, start families, and eventually gain visibility in professional or political arenas. After a period of time, which usually lasted several decades, each group of immigrants was judged to have successfully integrated into the mainstream and became hyphenated: Mexican-Americans, Japanese-Americans, or Chinese-Americans. Because assimilation revolves around power, however, descendants of white immigrants typically skip the hyphenation and are simply referred to as Americans.

The language that is used to talk about immigration reflects the power dynamic that underlies demands for assimilation. In the press, immigrants from former colonies or from poor countries are often indiscriminately referred to as "migrants" while immigrants from industrialized countries are called "expats." Britain, which has spent the last few years trying to break off from the European Union because it wanted more control over its borders, has the largest number of citizens living abroad compared to any other European country. These five million British citizens—retirees in Morocco or Cyprus, bankers in Paris or Frankfurt, hospitality workers in Dubai or Abu Dhabi—are often called, and call themselves, "expats."

When expats make the effort to learn the local language, adopt local customs, and dress in local garb, they are said to have "gone native." When migrants do it, they are still scrutinized for signs that might indicate whether they have "assimilated" sufficiently into the dominant group.

Expats aren't usually referred to as "illegal" or even "undocumented" when they overstay their visas. As many as one million Americans currently reside in Mexico, the vast majority of them—90 percent by one estimate—without residency papers, but the common term for them ("gringos") does not connote legality or precariousness. Immigrants who do this in the U.S. are routinely called "illegal aliens" or "removable aliens." Sometimes, the label "migrant" is applied even when the people in question are not immigrants at all, but refugees. In the summer of 2015, Syrians who were seeking asylum in the U.S. from a civil war that claimed half a million lives were sometimes inaccurately referred to by national news organizations and wire services as "migrants."

Immigrants continue to contribute to America in a million different ways, from growing the food on its tables to innovating the technologies its citizens use every day. Some are exceptional in their fields, while others work in the fields, doing jobs that few natives are willing to take because of their low wages. Whether documented or undocumented, immigrants commit far fewer crimes than native-born citizens. But whenever an offense, particularly a violent offense, involves immigrants, the entire project of immigration is called into question. *The problem is*, the nativists might say, *they don't assimilate*.

What about the cost of assimilation for an immigrant? If assimilation involves an individual becoming more similar to the group, then surely it must also mean that the individual renounces parts of herself in the process. Even under the best of circumstances, immigration is a traumatic experience that cuts a person's life into two: there is the life before and the life after. For the first year after I moved to the United States, I wore two watches, one that told the time in Los Angeles and the other the time in Rabat. In the morning, while I was getting ready for class, I would often think about my family six thousand miles away, sitting down to afternoon tea. In my memory, everyone back home remained exactly as I had last seen them, as if caught in a photograph. It never occurred to me that, day after day, they were getting older, making new friends, switching jobs, or moving house. They were changing, just as I was changing.

Whenever I stepped out of my apartment, I felt keenly aware that I was speaking a foreign language, whose sentences I had to compose with deliberation before I could speak them. In graduate seminars, my classmates would chuckle or even laugh when they heard me mispronounce some words, especially those I had only known in print—*epitome* and *fortuitous* and *onomatopoeia*. At times, the phonetic rules of English didn't make much sense to me: why did *rough* rhyme with *tough*, but not with *dough*? Eventually, I adapted to the local dialect and my foreign accent became less noticeable. One morning, a few years after arriving in this country, I woke up with the startling realization that I had dreamt in English.

Language was the easy part, however. There were so many cultural differences that hardly a day went by when I didn't notice a new one. It was not considered impolite, for example, to eat one's breakfast in front of others in the dorm's common room, without offering to share it with them. It was not considered rude to invite someone to lunch at a restaurant, and then expect them to pay for their meal. It seemed to me that Americans were always rushing around, never taking the time to sit down for a cup of coffee or a proper dinner. I was shocked the first time I saw a woman eating a hamburger as she drove down the 10 freeway. (If I sound singularly focused on food, perhaps it's because food is so intimately tied to culture.)

Some years later, I became an immigrant myself. Nothing could have prepared me for what I would gain—or for what I would lose. I missed my grandmother's funeral, four of my cousins' weddings, and countless birthdays and special celebrations with my family. If there was a crisis, I could never be sure that I would be there to help. Once, I remember, I was on vacation in Jackson Hole, Wyoming, when I received a text in the middle of the night telling me that my father was in the hospital and that he might not make it. He'd been suffering from a urinary-tract infection, whose symptoms he dismissed until it was too late; now he was showing signs of sepsis. For several minutes, my mind couldn't comprehend the text I was reading. All I wanted then was a chance to say goodbye. But, as I quickly found out, flights from LAX to Casablanca were fully booked, and the only itinerary I could find—with a stopover in Europe—was expensive. I made it work, somehow, and flew back. To my relief, the treatment he received worked and, while he slowly recovered, we had a chance to spend some time together. But the fear I experienced that summer stayed with me. I suspect it's a fear that every immigrant has: that text, that phone call telling you that a family member thousands of miles away is ill.

Of course, these experiences are not unusual; I share them with nearly 40 million people in the United States. All immigrants walk around with a scar left behind by their crossing into a new country, an invisible mark of the exile that became their condition when they were uprooted. Their children grow up without grandparents, without aunts and uncles and cousins, without a reservoir of collective family memory passed down through generations. While immigrants nurse this immense loss, they are told that they must adjust and belong by giving up even more of their culture. If they cling to a mode of dress, a language, or a habit that seems too conspicuous to the majority, they might be told that they are not assimilating, or not assimilating enough. They live their lives in the particular, but find it reflected back to them in the generic, whether in the speeches of ambitious politicians or in the plotlines of Hollywood movies. Their success is attributed to America, its countless opportunities, the uniqueness of its melting pot; their failure belongs only to their country of origin, their race, or their culture.

When I became an immigrant, I knew right away that my life would change. But I could never have expected that someday, while I sat on a plane to Reno, an old white man would grumble to me about the assimilation of *other* immigrants.

Complaints about assimilation are different from complaints about undocumented immigration, even though they're often spoken of in the same breath. The former are about identity; the latter are, strictly speaking, about legality. I remember an incident that took place at a garage sale my husband and I held some years ago, when we were living in Redondo Beach. We'd advertised it in the *Beach Reporter* and on brightly colored flyers posted on telephone poles all around the neighborhood, with the result that turnout was huge. Dozens of bargain hunters milled about, asking about the price of this or that item. "Cuanto quiere usted por el sofá?" an older gentleman asked me, pointing to our old green couch. The Spanish I had taken in college came in handy: I quoted him a price, adding, by way of explanation, "Es un sofá cama." Hearing our exchange, a white woman turned around and yelled at us, "Speak English! You're in America." I was stunned. "Hey—," I said, but she walked off, got into her car, and drove down the street, trailing a cloud of gas exhaust.

At the time, I didn't understand why it had bothered this woman so much to hear two people speak Spanish—in California, of all places. How did our exchange affect her? It certainly didn't limit her ability to ask about items on sale or to make a purchase of her own. When I told a friend about this incident, he wondered aloud if the woman's outburst was driven by worries about undocumented immigration. That spring, the state of California had been reeling from Prop. 187, the infamous ballot initiative championed by Governor Pete Wilson, which sought to deny unlawful immigrants, including children, access to state resources such as education and healthcare. (The law passed by a wide margin, but was struck down as unconstitutional.) However, the woman hadn't said anything about a scarcity of jobs or the use of public resources. She had expressed demands about how public space should be structured. In her view, English needed to retain its dominance in public and any breach of that rule could only be taken as evidence of a refusal to assimilate.

So challenges about assimilation are primarily about identity—a nebulous mix of race, religion, and language. People who perceive themselves to be under threat of losing their group dominance, and the privileges that come from it, aren't really concerned about jobs, a point that was amply illustrated by the 2016 presidential election. A survey by the Public Religion Research Institute and *The Atlantic* found that white working-class voters were 3.5 times more likely to support

Donald Trump if they reported feeling "like a stranger in their own land." My seatmate on the plane to Reno was a small-business owner, yet he did not seem worried about Korean-Americans taking opportunities away from him in Gardena; he seemed more aggrieved that their children studied two languages, or that his community featured store signs and church marquees in an alphabet he could not read. The loss of his cultural dominance was really what triggered his complaints. Others might object to their neighbors' wearing skullcaps, or eating fermented duck eggs, or listening to Tejano music, or any other cultural practices—and call these concerns about assimilation, too.

One reason that assimilation is continuously debated in America is that there is no consensus on whether it should be about principles or about identity. The multiculturalists would emphasize a belief in the Constitution and the rule of law, a commitment to pay taxes, a willingness to serve on juries or in public office or in the military. Where necessary, they support legislative changes to discourage ancestral customs among newcomers that might defy those values. For example, many states have passed legislation that makes it a felony to perform female genital mutilation on anyone under the age of eighteen. These laws are intended to deter the practice, still prevalent in certain parts of Africa and Asia, from being performed in the United States. (Only three cases have been reported in this country, and then swiftly prosecuted, in the past twenty years.)

But for the nativists, nothing short of the abandonment of all traces of one's heritage will do, a position that is tantamount to racial supremacy. Muslim women who wear the headscarf are often accused of not assimilating or, more egregiously, wanting others to assimilate to them. The perception that visible signs of religious identity are indicators of sinister splits in society can lead to rabid fears of wholly imaginary threats. In the last decade, more than fourteen states have enacted what came to be called "anti-Sharia measures," vaguely worded laws that prohibit the application of foreign legislation, under the rationale that Muslims will seek to impose their own religious laws on unsuspecting Americans. The fact that Muslims make up 1 percent of the U.S. population and that such an agenda is both a statistical and a constitutional impossibility has done nothing to temper this fear. In May 2015, more than two hundred armed activists showed up outside mosques in Phoenix, Arizona, to protest—well, it's unclear what they were protesting, other than the very presence of Muslims and their places of worship in their community. It is this form of assimilation, which demands complete subordination to the dominant culture and the expulsion of anyone perceived as different, that has been gaining ground in recent years.

The long history of immigration in the United States follows a well-established pattern: initial suspicion, a period of conflict and adjustment, and eventual integration into the mainstream. Adapting to a new culture is a process, not a switch. It takes years, maybe even decades, and involves adjustments on the part of the individual immigrant as well as the surrounding community. Nowadays, many Americans will wear green on St. Patrick's Day without thinking much about the periods during which the Irish were accused of contaminating the nation with their foreign habits. Yet each new generation thinks that the challenges it faces are unique and unprecedented: one often hears that "*this* group is different." There is no evidence that it is different. But because there is no objective measure of assimilation, many people end up throwing up their hands and saying "Well, I know it when I see it."

The question is: who gets to do the judging?

My seatmate on the plane to Reno seemed to believe that he did. "They don't assimilate," he'd decided about his Korean-American neighbors, even though the only evidence he could provide for this appraisal was Sunday-school classes. He is far from alone. Complaints about lack of assimilation frequently come from powerful men who speak as though they are neutral and final arbiters on the question. Donald Trump once said that assimilation of Muslims "has been very hard. It's almost—I won't say nonexistent, but it gets to be pretty close. And I'm talking about second and third generation. . . . For some reason, there's no real assimilation." John Kelly, the former secretary of homeland security, had a problem with undocumented immigrants from Latin America: in an interview with NPR, he said that "they're not people that would easily assimilate into the United States. They're overwhelmingly rural people. In the countries they come from, fourth, fifth, sixth-grade educations are kind of the norm. They don't speak English." More recently, the journalist Tom Brokaw expressed misgivings on *Meet the Press* about Latinx immigrants' ability to integrate in America: "The Hispanics should work harder at assimilation. That's one of the things I've been saying for a long time. They ought not to be just codified in their communities but make sure that all their kids are learning to speak English."

But these are not neutral judgments, or even factual ones. With regard to the religion question, surveys have consistently shown that the overwhelming majority of Muslim Americans feel pride in their national and religious identities, are satisfied with their lives, and believe in the national myth of the

American Dream. They display the same commitment to religion as Christians and attend religious services at the same rates as Christians. They rank being a good parent as a more important goal than leading a religious life or being successful, a choice that mirrors patterns among the general population. Although they report experiences of discrimination, the majority feel that non-Muslims are either friendly or neutral toward them. Looking at the demographic data, and particularly the direction of trends over time, it's clear that the president's accusations against Muslims are politically convenient rather than factually correct.

As for the language question, while the rate of English proficiency among foreign-born Latinx has remained unchanged since 1980, proficiency among U.S.-born Latinx is at nearly 90 percent, a rate that is likely to grow even higher as these native-born citizens speak English to their children. This is a pattern that mirrors the language loss of every group of immigrants that has come to this country. If anything, the process may be faster during this generation than it was a couple of centuries ago, when there was no compulsory K–12 schooling or educational TV programming or ESL classes designed to help young learners with their language skills. In the past, language loss was a much slower process. Between the eighteenth and twentieth centuries, the German language continued to be spoken by German immigrants and their offspring in Pennsylvania, New York, and parts of the Midwest. There were German-language newspapers, and German was used in some schools. German-language use, at least in public, only began to decline during and after World War I.

It's also important to question why English-language proficiency—particularly monolingual English proficiency—is considered normal or desirable in the United States. In other multiethnic and multicultural nations, by contrast, bilingualism or even multilingualism is almost always the standard. The insistence on English proficiency for immigrants establishes a link between citizenship and linguistic origin, suggesting that the only legitimate way to be American is to speak English—and only English. Language loss is one area in which the effect of assimilation to white Protestant culture can be cruelly felt, with a resulting linguistic impoverishment for the nation as a whole.

As our plane approached the airport in Reno, my seatmate asked me whether I was going there for business or pleasure. "I'm giving a talk about one of my books," I said, and told him about the event, co-sponsored by Nevada Humanities and the Pulitzer Center, that was to take place that evening in town. "I've never met an author before," he said with a delighted smile. He asked me what my book was about; I said it was a novel based on the true story of the first African person to cross America. "That's fascinating. What's the title of your book?" he asked, as he pulled out a pen and a piece of paper. "I'm going to read it."

Tribe

"But why?" my daughter asked. I had just finished reading *Huckleberry Finn* to her and her face was still nestled against my shoulder. She'd been amused by Huck's mischief, his dress-up games, and his staunch resistance to the Widow Douglas's attempts to "sivilize" him, but it was Huck's relationship with Jim that had truly riveted her. For much of the story, Huck wrestles with whether he should help Jim escape from slavery—he doesn't want to commit a sin, or he's afraid of breaking the law, or he doesn't want to be alone—until the moment comes when he decides he will do the right thing even if it means he will "go to hell." By then, however, Jim has been captured, sold, and held on the Phelps plantation, which belongs to Tom Sawyer's family. With Huck's help, Tom concocts an elaborate scheme for Jim's release, including digging a tunnel and drawing a coat of arms on the wall of his cell, details that Tom picked up from reading adventure stories. "But why?" my daughter wanted to know when we finished the book. "Why didn't Tom tell Jim the truth—that Miss Watson had already freed him in her will?"

She was not alone in asking—scholars have long debated this question. I tried my best to give her an honest answer: *Huckleberry Finn* shows slavery through the eyes of a child, allowing readers to apprehend the depravity of the institution, but Mark Twain also asks them to confront the reality that even after Jim is free, he is not equal. Tom Sawyer dictates the terms of that freedom, prioritizing his own amusement over Jim's agony. That this scene takes place so late in the novel, after Jim has been shown to be a loving husband, a caring father, and a deeply moral man who is willing to sacrifice himself for "forty year" to keep Tom safe from harm only adds to the grisly picture that Twain has drawn of racial dynamics in America.

Nearly two hundred years have passed since the events depicted in *Huckleberry Finn*, but in many ways white identity still expresses itself through the assertion of power over black identity, and cannot be fully defined without it. *Identity* is a vexing word, I know. It is racial or sexual or national or religious or all those things at once. It is often said to be in crisis. Now and then it can be mistaken, or even stolen. Sometimes it is proudly claimed, other times it is hidden or denied. In politics, it is derided as the last refuge of unthinking voters. But what is remarkable about the term *identity* is that it's almost never applied to whiteness; racial identity is taken to be exclusive to black people and people of color. When American media organizations discuss race, it is usually in connection with African-Americans or Asian-Americans or indigenous people or some other group that has been designated a minority. "White" is seen as the default, the absence of race.

Examples of this asymmetry abound. In school curriculums, the month of February is reserved for the study of black history, while much of the year is devoted to plain history, with no overt markers to signal that the bulk of the figures being studied are white. The novelists Toni Morrison, Percival Everett, and Octavia Butler are frequently referred to as African-American writers, while Joyce Carol Oates, Cormac McCarthy, and Stephen King are simply American writers. A James Bond character is assumed to have global appeal when it is played by Daniel Craig, but its universality is called into question when the filmmakers consider Idris Elba for the role. Tourists might speak of their travels to the Dark Continent, but no one says they've spent the summer backpacking through the Light Continent. People will tell you they are fans of black or Latin music; few will claim they love white music.

Whiteness, then, is shrouded in silence. To speak about it openly is to break a taboo. I've often noticed the physical discomfort—shifting eyes, a change in posture, an abrupt redirecting of the conversation—that the mere mention of whiteness can cause in many white people. Because they are not used to discussing their race, much less having it discussed by others, they do not know how to go about it, and so it is easier to avoid the subject altogether. The blog *Stuff White People Like*, which was created in 2008 and which listed activities such as yoga, camping, and going to farmers' markets, was from its inception presented as humor. "This is hilarious," the author told a bookstore audience when the blog was sold to a major publisher and released as a book, "this is so funny, this is great." Presenting whiteness otherwise—that is, as a serious subject of discussion—still causes a great deal of apprehension.

Every once in a while, the pervasive silence on whiteness is disrupted by an unexpected occurrence. The election of Donald Trump was exactly such an event. A real-estate magnate and reality-television star with no political experience, Trump managed to earn the votes of a majority of white people in America by running a campaign that appealed directly to their anxiety. To be clear, there is nothing particularly new about convincing white voters that people of other races represent a threat. In 1976, Ronald Reagan delivered outraged soliloquies about the "welfare queen," an unspecified "woman in Chicago" who had "eighty names, thirty addresses, twelve Social Security cards," collected veterans' benefits on "four non-existing deceased husbands," and made $150,000 in tax-free income every year. Four years later, he ran for the presidency again, this time with the slogan *Let's Make America Great Again*, and won in a landslide. In 1988, a political action committee working to elect George H. W. Bush ran television ads about Willie Horton, a black felon who committed assault and rape while on a furlough program supported by Bush's opponent, Massachusetts governor Michael Dukakis. In 1992, while he was campaigning for the Democratic nomination, Bill Clinton played a round of golf, to which television reporters were invited, in a whites-only club in Little Rock, Arkansas, and made a special trip to his home state in order to oversee the execution of Ricky Ray Rector—a brain-damaged black man whose mental state should have earned him a reprieve from capital punishment. In 2000, allies of George W. Bush's presidential campaign sent emails and distributed flyers in South Carolina claiming that John McCain, his rival for the Republican nomination, had "sired" a child outside marriage—specifically, a "Negro child." McCain had been ahead by double digits in the polls, but he lost the South Carolina primary, and eventually the nomination, to Bush.

But to say that something is not new does not mean that it should be accepted or sanctified. And while Trump is part of a long tradition, two things distinguish him from his predecessors. First, his run for the presidency not only followed the election of America's first black president, but was almost entirely predicated upon it. Trump was an early proponent of the birther conspiracy theory, and it's in large part thanks to it that, as early as 2011, he began his transformation from business celebrity to political commentator, invited to offer his opinions on talk shows across the political spectrum, from Fox News's *Laura Ingraham Show* to NBC's *The View*. Second, Trump is blunt and vulgar. What others convey as subtext, he presents as text. Immigration must be reformed, he said, to prevent Mexican "rapists" and "drug dealers" from coming here. Terrorism could be stopped through a "complete and total shutdown of Muslims." The big banks would not be held in check by his Democratic opponent, whose picture he tweeted alongside a Star of David. Jobs were disappearing from America because of bad trade deals with China, which was "raping our country." Football players who kneel in protest of police brutality, he told a rally in Alabama, were "sons of bitches" who should be "taken off the field." The consistent message, both during his campaign and during his presidency, is that America is in danger from various Others. The only constituency that Trump never faults for anything are whites. These people he speaks of as victims of a system that is rigged against them. In so doing, he gives voice to white anxiety.

At the heart of this anxiety is an increasing awareness on the part of white people that they will become a demographic minority in this country within a generation. The paradox is that they have no lexicon to speak about their own identity. *White* is a category that has afforded them an evasion from race, rather than an opportunity to confront it. To talk about white historical figures critically in schools—figures such as Christopher Columbus, Thomas Jefferson, or Andrew Jackson—is to saddle white children with the knowledge that their ancestors did not merely participate in the exploration, establishment, and expansion of the United States, but also in the genocide, enslavement, and subjugation of tens of millions of people, a process that accrued social, political, and economic benefits for the white majority. This knowledge is considered too heavy a burden. Instead, during the month of February, American children are taught inspirational stories about black historical figures—Harriet Tubman, Rosa Parks, or Martin Luther King, Jr.—who triumphed over injustice. The perpetrators and beneficiaries of that injustice remain largely unnamed. Whiteness is therefore perceived, experienced, and passed down as silence.

This silence has a terrible cost. White supremacists exploited it in the 1980s when they began using expressions like "white pride" and "white heritage," which deliberately echoed terms conceived by black civil rights leaders to celebrate and empower cultures that had been erased or denigrated for several centuries. Because the history of race begins with the subjugation of one group by a more politically powerful group, the appropriation of terms like "white pride" and "white heritage" became a message to white people that they should see themselves as a racial community fighting for its own advancement to equality. The fact that nearly all political, economic, and cultural power in the United States lies in the hands of white elected representatives, business executives, and board administrators did not disturb this logic in the least.

Two other descriptors for the experience of whiteness, which were introduced by academics, recently entered the mainstream and have become hotly contested as a result. One is the term "white privilege," which was coined in 1988 by the feminist scholar Peggy McIntosh to describe a range of systemic unearned advantages that benefit white people—from significant experiences, like being confident that she will be able to rent or buy a house in an area she can afford, to less significant ones, like speaking with her mouth full and not having anyone assume it is connected to her race. The second term is "white fragility," which was introduced by the critical discourse scholar Robin DiAngelo to refer to the range of angry or defensive reactions that even a minimal exposure to racial stress triggers in white people. As a workplace sensitivity trainer, DiAngelo noticed a pattern: many white people believed themselves to be *individually* free of racism and resented having to hear about their profiting from its *systemic* aspects—school segregation, pay discrimination, housing loan inequities, and so on. When confronted by evidence of racism, they might say "*I* don't see color" or "*I* was raised to treat everyone the same."

The two terms have been derided as exemplars of political correctness, even as a form of racism, because they ascribe group attributes to individuals without basis. But racism is not simply a matter of applying labels—if all we needed to do to stop racism was to use certain labels and avoid others, then defeating it would be relatively straightforward. Racism is a system that gives members of the dominant group both immediate and generational benefits that are not accessible to members of non-dominant groups. Those benefits accrue even when there is anti-discrimination legislation in place. For example, a 1988 investigative report by Bill Dedman of the *Atlanta Journal-Constitution* showed that, notwithstanding the Fair Housing Act, black applicants were turned down for home loans twice as often as white applicants, and that high-income blacks were rejected at the same rates as low-income whites. In the thirty years since, a wealth of sociology research has demonstrated that, controlling for factors such as poor credit history or amount of debt, mortgage approval rates for whites and non-whites continue to differ.

The other common objection to the concept of white privilege is that it doesn't apply to all white people. Some white people, particularly the poor and the poorly educated, face daunting obstacles to economic or educational achievement and thus feel unfairly targeted by the term. A white high school dropout in a derelict mill town might look around and ask, in bewilderment, *What privilege do I have?* Others, like white immigrants, make the case that they have derived no generational advantages from race, given their recent arrival in the United States. But white privilege doesn't mean that white people have easy lives—it simply means that whiteness does not make their lives harder. Blackness, by contrast, has a statistically measurable and negative effect on the outcome of individual efforts in employment, housing, and education. In a groundbreaking study in 2003, the sociologist Devah Pager showed that black job seekers are less than half as likely to be considered for employment as white job seekers with the same qualifications, and that white job seekers *with felony convictions* still fare better than black job seekers with no criminal record. A recent study by the Economic Policy Institute showed that black male college graduates earn 20 percent less than white male college graduates, and the disparity grows as incomes rise. Whiteness grants its holder a starting advantage that other races simply don't have.

The dispute over the proper language to talk about whiteness illustrates the paradox I mentioned earlier. If whiteness is claimed as a source of pride ("white power"), it calls back to centuries of colonialism, genocide, and dispossession in this country. If it is criticized for the advantages it grants ("white privilege"), it triggers denials or defensive responses. The resistance, particularly in conservative circles, to the term "white privilege" stems from the perception that white people are being singled out for opprobrium they feel they do not deserve—in other words, they're being treated as "bad." This is a form of shaming, they believe, and can only further divide a society already riven by tribalism. Racism is a system, however. In discussing it, it's not particularly useful to focus on individual racists as bad people and individual non-racists as good people. In any case, bad people can suffer from racism, just as good people can benefit from it. Eradicating racism in American society is not about turning bad people into good people—an ambition that I think is best left to faith leaders. It is about ensuring that everyone is treated equally, which is a basic duty of a democratic government toward its citizens.

When I moved to the United States, I supported myself by teaching Arabic and French to undergraduate students. I was asked to fill out a great many forms—what my graduate school classmates delightfully, if mysteriously, called "paperwork." Several of these forms included a section about race. I think there were five categories in those days: American Indian or Alaska Native; Asian; Black; Native Hawaiian or Pacific Islander; and White. Some of these categories were based on geography, and therefore easy enough to interpret, but others were more broadly about skin color. On the back of the form, definitions of each category were provided. "White" applied to "a person having origins in any of the original peoples of Europe, the Middle East, or North Africa" while "Black" applied to "a person having origins in the black racial groups of Africa."

I was bewildered, both by the imperative to self-identify and by the narrowness of the categories on the list. Where would Moroccans fit in such categories? Someone who was born in the north of Morocco, say, and had ancestry in one of the tribes from the Rif Mountains, would have to check the "White" box, while someone from the south of Morocco, with ancestry in any of the tribes from the Sahara, would have to check the "Black" box. What about those who, like me, were from the middle part of the country? And what of the complication that many Moroccans' self-perception is intimately tied to their ethnicity—Arab or Amazigh—or their religion—Muslim or Jewish?

After a few minutes of confusion, I checked both the White and Black boxes, in the hope that this somehow conveyed the fact that I was brown. It felt strange to have to fill out the form, knowing that, when I stepped out of the linguistics department's office, I would become part of how America sorted, counted, and conceived of itself. Later that afternoon, I ran into Abdessalam, a fellow Moroccan student in the same program, on the steps of Grace Ford Salvatori Hall. He was Afro-Arab, and I was curious what box he'd checked on the form when he'd filled it out the year before. "White," he told me with a laugh. "That's how they count us." Then we both shook our heads at the absurdity of the situation. This is not to say that there was no racial paradigm in our native country, but it is to say that neither of us had thought of racial identity as a single box to be checked. At the time, I resented being forced to fill out the forms; they seemed invasive and unnecessary.

But as months and then years went by, I saw how these forms, imperfect as they may have been, were used to track all kinds of interactions between the state and its citizens— enrollment in public schools and universities; treatment in health clinics and hospitals; enlistment in the armed services; granting of real-estate loans; and outcomes of encounters with police. These data give relatively objective measures of current inequalities in American society. For example, black and

Hispanic students graduate from college at lower rates than white and Asian students; the indigenous infant mortality rate is far higher than the white infant mortality rate; and black and Hispanic enlistment in the armed forces is higher than their participation in the labor force. In other words, the statistical data on race provided transparency. And part of what makes the conversation on racial identity uncomfortable for so many people is the fact that transparency leads to accountability.

After I became a citizen I thought, somewhat naïvely I admit, that I would be treated no differently than other Americans. Since then, however, I have had ample opportunity to see all the ways in which this was not true. Two weeks after the 2016 election, when I wrote about white identity politics for the *New York Times*, a reader replied, "You didn't stay in Morocco but moved to the UK/USA built by whites, use them, yet blame them. Such blatant hypocrisy." This man was simultaneously ignorant of the fact that these two countries were built with the labor of colonized and enslaved people, and indignant that I dared to have opinions about the nation to which I had sworn allegiance. My citizenship is also called into question whenever I object to the U.S. occupations of Afghanistan and Iraq or its airstrikes in Pakistan or Yemen. On social media, criticism of American foreign policy frequently earns me responses of "Go back to your country."

The demand to "go back," which is sometimes phrased as "love it or leave it," rests on the assumption that the archetypal American is white—an idea that dates back to the earliest days of the nation. The Naturalization Act of 1790 limited citizenship to "free white persons" who had lived in this country for at least two years. The residency requirement was extended twice—to five years in 1795 and to fourteen years in 1798—but whiteness continued to be a condition for citizenship. In 1848, after the Mexican-American war ended, the Treaty of Guadalupe Hidalgo brought large swaths of southwestern territory into the Union and extended U.S. citizenship to Mexican-Americans. Yet citizenship remained contested. In 1857, the Supreme Court ruled in *Dred Scott* that neither slaves nor their descendants could be citizens, because the mores of the time as well as the language in the Declaration of Independence made clear that they were "beings of an inferior order." It took the Civil War and the passing of the Fourteenth Amendment in 1868 for citizenship to be extended to black people: "all persons born or naturalized in the United States, and subject to the jurisdiction thereof, are citizens."

Although the language of the amendment seems clear, it didn't entirely settle the legal status of everyone born in the United States, as the Wong Kim Ark case soon showed. Wong, a cook who had been born to temporary workers in San Francisco, was denied re-entry to the U.S. after a trip to China in 1894, on the grounds that he was not a citizen and was therefore subject to the Chinese Exclusion Act that had been passed by Congress just two years earlier. With help from a Chinese benevolent association, he sued the federal government, and in 1898 the Supreme Court ruled in his favor, firmly establishing the principle of birthright citizenship: any person born in the United States was a citizen, regardless of the ethnic origin or legal status of the parents. However, indigenous people were still members of sovereign nations and remained ineligible for citizenship. Natives who were taxed, served in the military, or married white people could apply for citizenship, but this was only granted on an individual basis. It was not until 1924, through an act of Congress, that Native citizenship in the United States was established.

But while access to citizenship was slowly being expanded

to nonwhites, it was incrementally restricted in other ways. The aforementioned Chinese Exclusion Act, which barred Chinese workers from entering the United States altogether, served to limit the pool of nonwhite children who could be born in the United States, and therefore become citizens. (Exclusion of Chinese people did not end until the Second World War, when political alliances became necessary to defeat Nazism.) The Immigration Act of 1924 established national-origin quotas that favored immigrants who came from northern European countries, and restricted those from eastern Europe, southern Europe, Asia, and Africa. Whiteness continued to be a condition of immigration and/or naturalization, in one form or another, until 1965.

In this context, it is not insignificant that Donald Trump's signature policy promise was a "total and complete shutdown of Muslims entering the United States." Before this pledge, he had been trying to distinguish himself from other Republican hopefuls in a crowded primary field. But afterward, he enjoyed a healthy bump in the polls and doubled down on his promise despite criticism from rivals as well as allies, including his eventual running mate, Mike Pence. The Muslim ban ensures that, for the foreseeable future, there will be no new Americans of Somali, Yemeni, Libyan, Iranian, or Syrian descent. Not coincidentally, people from these countries are widely considered nonwhite or else insufficiently white. Given the history of citizenship, the rhetoric of the president, and the fact that no national from these countries perpetrated an attack on U.S. soil in the forty years preceding the policy, the immigration ban can only be interpreted as another attempt to maintain white demographic dominance.

· · ·

Because full citizenship is still a privilege of whiteness, white people can often rely on the state to act on their behalf against nonwhites—that is, against conditional citizens. Consider interactions in public spaces, where people of all racial identities have, since desegregation at least, the same legal right to appear and move about. In May 2018, a white lawyer went on a public rant in a Manhattan deli, berating the restaurant workers for speaking Spanish. "I pay for their welfare," he said. "I pay for their ability to be here. The least they can do is speak English." Then he threatened to report them to Immigration and Customs Enforcement. Earlier that month, a white student reported a black student for taking a nap in the common room of their dorm at Yale, saying, "I have every right to call the police—you cannot sleep in that room." Also that month, a white mother called the police about two Native American students taking part in a campus tour at Colorado State University, telling the dispatcher that "they are not, definitely not, a part of the tour."

The language in these complaints—"I pay," "I have every right," "they are definitely not"—is illuminating. It indicates a belief on the part of these white people that they are the custodians of public space and can enlist the police to enforce its boundaries. Such incidents were by no means unusual. That year, there were numerous reports of white people calling the police on black people and people of color for arbitrary reasons: waiting too long at a Starbucks in Philadelphia, having a barbecue on Lake Merritt in Oakland, playing a leisurely round of golf at a club in Pennsylvania, or checking out of an Airbnb in Rialto, California. Once police officers arrived, their responses ranged from an arrest on charges of trespassing, which is how the incident at the Starbucks in Philadelphia ended, to the installation of a perimeter and the arrival of a police helicopter, which is what happened after the encounter at the Airbnb in Rialto.

In public spaces, particularly those that might be characterized as elite, white presence is treated as ordinary and invisible, whereas the presence of nonwhites is not only visible, but monitored. Speaking a language other than English, at a volume higher than a whisper, might draw confrontations about immigration status, as happened in the Manhattan deli incident. Speaking a non-dominant variety of English can lead to challenges about qualifications, or it can be perceived, in and of itself, as a marker of poor education. A few months before the Manhattan deli incident, the *Washington Post* reported that the Department of Education had handed out a checklist to its employees to help them identify bomb threats made over the phone. The list included identifiers about tone of voice, background noise, and spoken language, including such indicators as "well-spoken," "educated," "Ebonics," "foul," "irrational," "incoherent," "taped," "read by threat," and "nervous." The use of Ebonics—or African-American Vernacular English, as linguists refer to it—was the only overt marker of race or ethnicity on the list, and its appearance, between "educated" and "foul," was clearly meant to suggest low education or offensive speech, despite the fact that AAVE is simply one English dialect among others, and millions of Americans, of different levels of education, code-switch in and out of it at will.

The stigmatization of non-dominant languages in the United States starts at an early age. When our daughter was three years old, my husband and I moved the family to Casablanca for a year. We had two reasons for the move: one was that I needed to do research for one of my books and the other was that we wanted our daughter to get an immersive language experience to help her become bilingual more quickly. By the time we returned to California, she was fluent in Arabic. On her first playdate with a friend from her new school in Los Angeles, I watched her try to teach him the word for apple: *tuffaaha*. But within weeks, she stopped speaking Arabic. It didn't matter what I tried, she wanted to speak English, like everyone else at her preschool. Even at four years old, she had somehow understood that the use of a different language in public space was a negative marker of difference, and she decided to give it up in order to feel a greater sense of belonging.

More recently, I was sitting in a waiting lounge at Los Angeles International Airport, speaking in Arabic to my sister on the phone. Across from me was a middle-aged white couple— a wholly unremarkable fact, except that the man kept looking worriedly at me every few minutes. Eventually, his eyes drifted to my T-shirt, which was emblazoned with the name of a popular musical act, and I saw him relax a little, though he still kept looking over. When my husband came back from the coffee stand with our drinks, I got off the phone and started talking to him—in English. Only then did the observer return to his magazine. In the United States, travelers are regularly instructed that they should "See Something, Say Something." Given that the presence of nonwhites is more visible in public spaces, it follows that this rule will be used more frequently to target nonwhites.

In theory, public space belongs equally to everyone. But identity markers like race and language affect the level of comfort and, in some cases, the physical safety of conditional citizens. A friend of mine, a black art historian, once told me that even when he is late to class or to a meeting, he never runs across the subterranean parking lot of his office building, because he is excruciatingly aware of how he might be perceived by others. The fear of having the police called on one for no reason is a reality that many black people and people of color have to live with in this country, and it is not new. But smartphones with cameras have helped to document such incidents, and social media have brought them to immediate and national attention. As a result, the assertion of white authority over public space now occasionally comes with the cost of social shaming.

A common refrain in the days after Trump's victory was "But not all his voters are racist." Opinion writers of different political persuasions declared that working-class people had legitimate "economic grievances," which Trump had been the only candidate willing to address. There was a whiff of elite blame to these pronouncements: the country had ended up with Trump because of ignorant working people. Conveniently, this position made racism a problem exclusive to the working class. As it happens, I come from the working class, back in Morocco. Neither of my parents finished high school, but they managed to buy a home and put their children through college—an arc of social mobility that was common in the United States as well. Increasingly, however, it is becoming rare. Unions have been gutted, and jobs that once enabled class advancement are now scarce. Trade deals like NAFTA have decimated entire towns, with the result that many people have become stuck in cycles of poverty and substance abuse. These workers have the cruel sense of being forgotten by the political class and condescended to by the cultural one.

But the argument that economic grievances drove working-class voters to Trump is not borne out by the evidence. The working class is not a monolith. By wide margins, black and Hispanic working-class voters chose Hillary Clinton, even though they presumably have the same economic worries as white working-class voters. It's important to remember, too, that white working-class voters chose a candidate who specifically promised them relief from their problems at the expense of other races. Even though their lives are difficult, they have the expectation, like Tom Sawyer in *Huckleberry Finn*, that they can still assert their authority and dictate the terms of others' freedom. That is a form of power, perhaps the only one they feel they still have.

If whiteness is no longer the default and is to be treated as a racial identity—even, as Trump wants it to be, a "minority"—then perhaps it is time white people considered what this might mean in practice. In November 2015, Robert L. Dear, an art dealer who called himself a "warrior for the babies," opened fire in the lobby of a Planned Parenthood in Colorado Springs, killing three patients and injuring nine. Two years later, Stephen Paddock, a professional gambler, checked into a room on the thirty-second floor of the Mandalay Bay Resort and Casino, and from his window opened fire on concertgoers at the Harvest Music Festival on the Las Vegas Strip, killing 58 people and causing another 851 to be injured. And on Valentine's Day in 2018, Nikolas Cruz, a GED student whose social media accounts included anti-black, anti-Semitic, and anti-Muslim slurs, opened fire inside Marjory Stoneman Douglas High School in Parkland, Florida, killing 17 of his former schoolmates and injuring another 17.

Had these mass murderers been perceived or treated as members of their race, then white people in America would have been lectured for weeks on end about religious and cultural tolerance, and called upon, as a community, to denounce the extremists in their midst. I recall a dinner conversation in December 2015, during which a friend of mine suggested that Muslim Americans needed a new strategy for dealing with violence perpetrated by Muslim terrorists. This was a week after a married Pakistani-American couple, Syed Rizwan Farook and Tashfeen Malik, burst into the Inland Regional Center in San Bernardino during an office Christmas party and fired their semiautomatic weapons, killing 14 people inside and injuring another 22. "What new strategy?" I asked him. "Muslim Americans need to enlist in the armed forces," he replied, arguing that it would demonstrate their patriotism to the general public, just as Japanese Americans had done during the Second World War. For the rest of the evening, I puzzled over this suggestion, which implied that Muslim Americans were not American by virtue of their birth; they had to earn the right, through military service, to be called Americans. The suggestion was all the more outlandish because Muslims have in fact served in every U.S. war since the Revolutionary War. But it was a sad reminder, from a friend no less, that Muslims were assumed to have a collective responsibility for the mass shooting in San Bernardino.

No such responsibility is placed on the shoulders of white people when a white man commits a similar crime. Each of the white shooters I mentioned was, instead, the subject of newspaper profiles that explored his mental health, family situation, and personal challenges. The *New York Times* reported that Robert Dear was "a gentle loner who occasionally unleashed violent acts towards neighbors." (Following public outcry, the *Times* rewrote the lead to the article before it went to press.) The *Los Angeles Times* described Paddock as a "loner" who liked to gamble, but "held steady jobs." The *Sun-Sentinel* wrote about the "slight" frame of Nikolas Cruz, his developmental challenges, and the bullying he had been subjected to in school. In other words, each of the shooters was treated as an individual, rather than as a representative of his identity group, and the national conversation that followed the attacks was not about failures of the white culture, but about the lack of mental healthcare in this country and the urgent need for gun legislation.

Similarly, the opioid epidemic in today's rural white communities is being treated very differently from the crack epidemic in urban black communities in the 1980s. Back then, the state's response was to expand police presence and to pass draconian criminal legislation, like three-strikes laws and mandatory minimum sentencing. An entire generation of black men and women was sent to prison for substance abuse. Nowadays, though, the government's approach to opioid addiction is to treat it as a public health issue, with state politicians asking for federal funding for drug treatment and counseling. This is a good development—drug addiction *should* be treated as a disease—but the different response only serves as evidence that, despite the fact that Donald Trump disturbed the silence on whiteness, white Americans can still largely escape the disadvantages of race.

Race is a fiction. Although it was built on observable geographical variations in skin tone, nose shape, or hair type, it has no biological basis. It was created for political and economic reasons, deployed as a means of obtaining free labor in perpetuity, and used to entrap hundreds of millions of people in a system that denied them freedom and human rights for many generations. Race is a seductive fiction. It ensnares both the dominant and non-dominant groups into a narrative that they can scarcely escape, reinforced as it is by the culture, a narrative that teaches them that their success or failure is due exclusively to their individual efforts and that history plays no part in it.

But race is also an elastic fiction. Whiteness, for example, is not a rigid or fixed category. The Naturalization Act of 1790, which applied to "free white persons," primarily advanced people of Anglo-Saxon background, but as immigrants from other parts of Europe, North Africa, and the Middle East began to migrate to the United States, the definition of "white" became narrower. The Johnson-Reed Act of 1924 limited immigration of southern Europeans, eastern Europeans, and other people who were considered insufficiently white. Members of these groups faced severe educational, social, and employment discrimination for decades. New York businesses posted employment notices advising that no Italians need apply. Ivy League universities established unspoken quotas to limit the admission of Jews. But it's worth remembering that Italians and Jews did not have to drink from separate fountains and were not confined to reservations. Even within the periphery of whiteness, they still had advantages over other nonwhites in the United States.

Arabs occupy a liminal space in American definitions of whiteness. The Census Bureau counts us as white, yet we are treated as nonwhites in encounters with the state or its agents: extra screenings at ports of entry; removals from flights based on complaints by white passengers; additions to the No Fly List; surveillance by law-enforcement or intelligence agencies; and the recent travel ban that targets relatives abroad. Although these experiences are well documented, they are difficult to study and appraise because the government does not keep precise statistical data on Arabs. No special box means no specific data. Statisticians are forced to extrapolate numbers based on the information that people volunteer on the census form.

There is an interesting history behind the unsettled status of Arabs in the United States. Arab immigrants who came to this country from Syria, Lebanon, and Palestine in the late nineteenth century were eager to be counted as white because that was the only way to establish their eligibility for citizenship. The fact that most of them were Christians served to bolster their claims, as it quelled the usual complaints about assimilation into white Protestant society. Furthermore, their principal occupations—as peddlers, factory workers, and entrepreneurs—facilitated English-language learning and citizenship applications. Their legal status was initially decided in *Dow v. United States* in 1915. George Dow, a Syrian Christian immigrant living in South Carolina, was twice denied citizenship because of the color of his skin, which "was darker than the usual person of white European descent." In this view, whiteness was a matter of skin color. On appeal, however, he was granted citizenship based on the fact that several Syrian applicants had been previously approved and the opinion that "the inhabitants of a portion of Asia, including Syria, are to be classed as white persons." While granting George Dow's claims to whiteness—and therefore to citizenship—the court drew a line between Middle-Easterners and the "Asiatics" that Congress was trying to exclude through legislation. Geography, then, could override skin color.

However, matters became more complicated when Arab Muslims began to immigrate, and later to petition for citizenship. In 1942, the District Court for the Eastern District of Michigan denied citizenship to a Yemeni immigrant and Detroit resident by the name of Ahmed Hassan. After taking note of Hassan's skin, which was "indisputably dark brown in color," and his geographic origin, which was technically "outside the zone from which Asiatic immigration is excluded," the court decided that "Arabs as a class are not white and therefore not eligible for citizenship." The ruling cited religious dimensions to citizenship, finding that "it is well known that [Yemenis] are a part of the Mohammedan world and that a wide gulf separates their culture from that of the predominantly Christian peoples of Europe." In sum, access to whiteness depended on a specific combination of skin color, geography, and religion. So Arabs weren't white, after all.

Less than two years later, and with an eye to new political alliances in the Middle East, judicial opinion would change once again and Arabs would be deemed legally white. Mohamed Mohriez—a Muslim immigrant from Badan, in present-day Saudi Arabia, who had lived in the United States for more than twenty years—petitioned for citizenship in 1944. Judge Wyzanski, writing for the U.S. District Court in Massachusetts, granted the petition, citing the recommendation of the Immigration and Naturalization Service, the achievements of Arabs in science and philosophy, and the "vital interests [of the United States] as a world power." Race, it turns out, is above all a politically useful fiction.

By the 1990s, Arab-American grassroots activists were becoming increasingly aware that legal whiteness did not result in political or cultural whiteness, so they began to lobby for the addition of a separate identity box on the census. The campaign was unsuccessful, however. In 2010, they pushed for a write-in approach, urging members of their communities to select "Other" on the census form and write in "Arab." But the respondents who dutifully specified "Arab" were later told that they were counted as white, regardless of their ancestry.

Legally, then, Arabs are white. They are not entitled to special considerations such as federal protections or affirmative action programs. But in practice, Arabs are nonwhite, as evidenced by government programs that target them as a class, like the special registration of Arab and Muslim men following the September 11 attacks or the various surveillance programs to which they have been subjected for years. Culturally, too, they are treated as a separate race, hence their almost universal portrayal as villains or victims in popular media.

Of course, one doesn't need to be white to have privileges. American society has many overlapping hierarchies that must be navigated every day. The rich have significant privileges compared with the poor, men compared with women, able-bodied people compared with the disabled, thin people compared with fat, and heterosexuals compared with LGBTQ people. I will readily admit to many privileges myself. My family never goes hungry. I have a home and access to clean water. I have employer-provided healthcare. I've run across subterranean parking lots without fear of causing alarm. I've been stopped by the police for speeding, and the encounter did not result in violence on my body.

But I am also an Arab, an immigrant, and a Muslim—subject to the current rhetoric, and perhaps someday the laws, that Donald Trump has promoted. On the night of his election, I was in upstate New York, far away from my family. Speaking to them on the phone, I could hear the terror in my daughter's voice as the returns came in. The next morning, her friends at school were in tears. My daughter called on the phone, in panic. "He can't make us leave, right?" she asked. "We're citizens." My husband and I did our best to quiet her fears. No, we said. He cannot make you leave. But every time I have thought about this conversation—and I have thought about it dozens of times, in my sleepless nights since the election—I have felt less certain.

Caste

The carpet was green. I can still picture its exact shade, twenty-six years later. There was a gray sofa, a bookshelf, and a Formica table with four chairs. "Let me show you," the landlord said, even though I could see everything there was to see from the doorway. He walked past me, twisted a handle on the left-side wall, and pulled out a Murphy bed. Next, he showed me the bathroom, whose door grazed the edge of the toilet seat each time it was opened or closed. Then came the kitchen, which, he pointed out twice, had a bright window. The rent was $450 a month—half of what I was paid each month to teach foreign languages to undergraduates at the University of Southern California—and it was the cheapest furnished apartment I could find, after months of combing through the classified ads in the *Los Angeles Times*. I signed the lease.

Two weeks later, I brought my suitcases to the apartment, unpacked my clothes and books, and sat down on the sofa, easing my shoes off. Almost immediately I felt a mosquito bite my ankle, and slapped it. I was bit again a minute later, and realized it wasn't a mosquito, it was a flea. Where there is one flea, I thought, there must be others. A quick inspection revealed that the carpet was infested with them. The previous tenant had kept pets; now I had inherited their parasites. Over the next few weeks, I sprayed the carpet, sprinkled baking soda, vacuumed compulsively, yet the fleas always won the battles I waged against them. It was clear I needed help, though I never mentioned the problem to anyone because I was embarrassed by it. I'm not sure what shamed me more: the fleas, or the poverty they suggested.

In addition to the fleas, the previous tenant had bequeathed me a rice cooker in decent condition. I didn't know how to cook, but I could read and press buttons, so I managed to make white rice and steamed vegetables, which I ate for dinner several nights a week. It never occurred to me that this might be an unbalanced diet until a staffer in the linguistics lab where I did my research stopped me in the hallway and asked me if I was all right. "I'm perfectly fine," I replied. "You've lost so much weight," she said, shaking her head. It was true I had lost a few pounds, but her comment seemed to me meddlesome, even inappropriate. A few days later, while buying coffee at the 32nd Street market across from campus, I passed out. I was with a man I had just started dating. He tapped my cheeks, tried to revive me, but my body felt as heavy as lead and as light as cotton, all at once. Through the haze, I heard the cashier say he was calling an ambulance, and was jolted back to consciousness. I had basic student health coverage; I couldn't afford an ambulance. So I sat for a few minutes, drank the glass of water the store manager brought for me, and went home.

The drive from campus to my apartment was a short fifteen minutes, but the trip always offered some instruction on the city's past and present. Depending on the route I took, I passed by frat houses, liquor stores, the service employees union, and taquerias that advertised *tres por un dólar*, or else I drove past the Wilshire Boulevard Temple, the historic Hotel Normandie, and Korean supermarkets that had been damaged or destroyed

during the Los Angeles uprisings a year and a half earlier. On
the radio, Eddie Vedder sang in soulful baritone that he was
still alive, still alive. The AC in my car didn't work and, with
my window down, I could taste the dust and exhaust of a
metropolis rebuilding itself.

My apartment complex had twenty-eight units, spread out
on two floors around a courtyard. I got to know some of my
neighbors: there was Jean, an elderly woman who lived two
doors down from me; Robert and Sung-hee, a Korean war vet
and his wife, who had a one-bedroom upstairs; and Nick, a
staffer for the *Los Angeles Times,* who occupied one of the cor-
ner units. We were all on fixed incomes, all of us in various
states of poverty. But the hardship in which I lived—that of the
graduate student—held a certain mystique. It indicated that
the economic struggle would be short-lived, because a financially stable job awaited after graduation. That, at least, seemed
to be the common assumption among some of my friends at
school, who provided for their necessities by using credit cards.
Others borrowed money from their parents, a luxury I didn't
have. As a foreign student, I also had little access to credit, and
in any case graduation was years away in the future. I was far
too preoccupied with the present, like how to get rid of the
pests in the carpet. I didn't complain to the landlord. If anything, I blamed myself, because what was I expecting for $450
a month? Eventually, I found something that worked—Borax
salt, I believe—and got rid of the fleas for good.

It occurs to me now that poverty is often associated with
parasites—and not just in literal ways. In every election, I can
count on one or another politician to rail against people who
"live off" taxpayers' money, receiving food stamps, rent assis-

tance, or medical services while making no discernible effort to become self-sufficient. California, where I have lived more than half my life, is particularly hostile to the poor. Before he conjured up the "welfare queen" on the presidential campaign trail, Ronald Reagan had won the California governorship in 1966 on a promise to end "freeloading at the expense of conscientious citizens." At that time, the number of Californians who were benefiting from federal assistance—Aid to Families with Dependent Children, or AFDC—was growing by as many as 40,000 new recipients each month, according to a press estimate. One out of every thirteen Californians was receiving some form of government help. That statistic could be interpreted in different ways: unemployment was growing; or the state's cost of living had risen and wages were not keeping up; or changing sexual mores had led to higher divorce rates and elevated levels of poverty. Reagan's explanation was simply that people were getting help they did not need. In 1971, he tightened eligibility rules for welfare, dropping from the rolls people who had some employment income; lengthened state residency provisions; and required that welfare recipients allow access to their income tax records. That combination—tougher qualifications and state monitoring—set the tone for how the poor would be treated in the state.

Over the next two decades, California introduced a series of changes to shrink the pool of welfare applicants, limit the time they could be on the program, and screen them for fraud even before they could receive aid. Welfare fraud investigations included financial record checks, interviews with the applicant and/or family members, and unscheduled home visits. Although welfare fraud was a real problem, it took on mythical proportions, driven in part by sensational media coverage. In 1994, Governor Pete Wilson introduced electronic fingerprinting of welfare applicants, a process akin to booking a suspect charged with a crime. The fingerprinting program was supposed to cut fraud—duplicate applications, for example—but the amount of money recouped by the state was relatively minimal, while it cost millions of dollars to implement. (At that time, the state already spent $72 million a year, or about 10 percent of welfare funds, on fraud detection. The new requirement cost another $17 million a year.) In addition, welfare fraud was no longer treated as an administrative violation and was increasingly referred for criminal prosecution.

By the time the fingerprinting program was terminated—nearly seventeen years later—only 50 percent of people eligible for food stamps in California were receiving them, one of the lowest rates of participation in the country. But welfare recipients in the state still undergo a draconian screening process that includes submitting their names, addresses, and Social Security numbers, which are matched against financial records and state and federal law-enforcement databases. They must agree to a reduction or termination of grant if a partner moves in, if they receive additional support from another job or agency, if they are convicted of a crime, or if they are found to use drugs. They must be photographed. After they begin receiving welfare payments, they must fill out paperwork regularly to keep their eligibility current. Their information is made available to the police without warrant. These policies, the law professor Kaaryn Gustafson has argued, have blurred the lines between the welfare system and the criminal justice system. Welfare applicants are treated as potential criminals, and their lives are under a form of social control that resembles the social control of parolees.

I had no opinion on Pete Wilson while I lived in that apartment building in Koreatown; the governor was as remote to me as an actor in a drama series on television. But I wonder what my neighbor Jean, who lived on Social Security, thought about his increasingly cruel policies toward the poor. Often, I would see her carrying small grocery bags into the building, shuffling past the art deco water fountain that had long ago stopped working. The landlord gave her a discount on the rent, she told me once, and charged her with being his assistant. I doubted he needed her services, because he lived in the building himself and was much younger and sprightlier than her. Yet she took her role with great seriousness: she would knock on my door to let me know that the mail had arrived early or that the dryer in the laundry room was broken. She was always in the mood for a chat, whether about the litter of cats that appeared one morning under the awning or about the Nancy Kerrigan/Tonya Harding controversy.

That year, Pete Wilson was running for re-election. He became, rather famously, a vocal supporter of Prop. 187, a ballot initiative that sought to deny undocumented immigrants access to public education and healthcare. Undocumented immigrants made up a sizable portion of laborers in the state's lowest-paying jobs: fruit and vegetable pickers, meatpackers, construction workers, and service workers. The ballot initiative would have set up a citizenship screening system that would have forced these workers' children out of school and denied them medical care. Like Wilson's welfare policy, this immigration proposal was premised on costly policing and punishment, an approach that would prove wildly popular with California voters. Yet I cannot recall seeing the governor or his surrogates campaigning anywhere in our neighborhood. If there were rallies, or canvassing efforts, or even posters and yard signs, I failed to see them.

.   .   .

Historically, the political elite in the United States has always regarded the poor with suspicion. At the founding of the nation, for example, voting was a privilege accorded exclusively to propertied white men. The justification for the restriction— inherited from English common law—was that ownership of property resulted in independence of means and therefore independence of decision-making, whereas being poor meant being subject to the whims of others. Property requirements were loosened incrementally and then abolished during the first half of the nineteenth century, as an increasing number of white men lived in cities or on the frontier, where they could make a living without owning property, but other restrictions aimed at the very poor, such as denying paupers the vote, continued for decades.

Inherent in these restrictions on class were restrictions on race and gender: white men had a say in how the country was to be run, whereas white women, indigenous people, free blacks, enslaved men and women, and immigrants of all backgrounds did not. However, the passing of the Fifteenth Amendment in 1870 meant that black men gained access to the ballot. Almost immediately, the political elite in the South used social class to prop up the crumbling edifice of white supremacy. Southern state legislatures circumvented the Fifteenth Amendment through a variety of tactics, including the imposition of poll taxes. Although poll taxes applied equally to black and white voters in the South, some states added grandfather clauses to their laws, exempting anyone whose grandparent had voted in an election prior to the Civil War from having to pay. The result was that poll taxes maximally affected black men. As for the poor whites who were denied the vote despite the use of grandfather clauses, they were considered disposable, a small sacrifice in the cause of white supremacy. By 1902, poll tax laws were firmly in place across the South.

In the North, meanwhile, new laws were passed—tax-payment requirements, literacy tests, and pre-election registration—that disproportionately affected poor voters. These laws, too, had racial dimensions, as they hampered foreign-born citizens who did not speak English or native citizens who did not speak it well enough. Then the secret ballot replaced the viva voce ballot, a move that provided privacy, but added a complication for voters with limited education, many of them poor. The logic that poor people were unfit to vote because they relied on others for their livelihoods was also applied to women, who were considered too dependent on their husbands, either materially or emotionally, to make rational political choices. It was not until after the First World War that suffragists had enough momentum to secure a constitutional amendment on women's vote, which was ratified in 1920. But black women remained subject to the same racist restrictions—disguised as class restrictions—that had been placed on black men in the South.

Poll taxes were abolished in 1964 and race-based restrictions in 1965, but the right to vote continues to be suppressed in different ways, with disproportionate effects on poor people. Election days are held on weekdays, which means that a huge number of American voters—hourly wage workers, independent contractors, temporary employees—face a choice between an election ballot and a reduced paycheck. Because wealth is not evenly distributed across races in the United States, class constraints on the vote tend to have similar outcomes as race constraints. The voter ID laws that have been passed in

Republican-held state legislatures since the early 2000s have also placed legal and financial burdens on suffrage that target the poor, with disproportionate effects on black, Hispanic, and indigenous voters.

Each era brings new ways to disempower the poor. Ten years ago, the Supreme Court ruled in *Citizens United* that associations of individuals (such as corporations) were as entitled to free speech as individuals, and that their financial spending on political campaigns constituted a form of speech. Supporters of *Citizens United* argue that the ruling is ideologically neutral because it applies to corporations and labor unions alike. However, union membership has dropped dramatically over the last fifty years, for reasons ranging from state laws that curtail union power to increasing globalization and automation. There are fewer workers in unions today than at any time since the 1930s. For this reason, political spending by unions is simply no match for spending by corporations. In any case, a dollar is not a word. In equating the two, the Court decided that ideas backed by the rich have more political value than those that are not, and in the process it handed corporations an overwhelming advantage in influencing government.

The electoral system works against the interests of the poor in many other ways. There is no federal public financing of elections, so it is virtually impossible for a person with an income at the poverty level (roughly $12,000 for an individual living alone) to afford the time it would take to run for and win public office. Part of what made Alexandria Ocasio-Cortez's election victory in 2018 against a ten-term incumbent in New York's 14th Congressional District so revolutionary was that she worked as a bartender and financed her campaign exclusively through individual contributions. But for every Ocasio-Cortez, there are dozens of Michael McCauls. (The representative from Texas's 10th Congressional District is reportedly worth $143 million.)

The disempowerment of the poor is both historical fact and current reality. It remains accepted in the culture because of the national myth that poverty is entirely under an individual's control. If you are poor, the thinking goes, it must be because you're not working, or not working hard enough, or not working long enough, or you're married to the wrong person, or have too many kids, or spend money on the wrong things, or you didn't go to college, or you went to college, but studied the wrong subject, or you studied the right subject, but took on too many loans. Even as empirical data consistently prove otherwise, class is taken to be the exclusive outcome of personal choices. It's for this reason that the rich are admired, while the poor are blamed.

This attitude is peculiarly American, I think. Growing up in Morocco—a country that is considered poor, at least according to indexes like nutrition levels, child mortality, and standard of living—I never got the sense that the neediest among us were to blame for their economic situation. Class was perceived to be the result of several factors, principally the family you were born into and its connections to the king and the nobility; the region you lived in; and your access to elite education, especially in French, the language of the former colonizing power. I witnessed both complete destitution and extreme wealth every day, side by side, in my extended family and in my social circle.

At Dar Es-Salam, the public high school I attended, my classmates included the offspring of government ministers and captains of industry as well as students who lived in a nearby slum. The disparities were clear from the moment the bell rang—some arrived in chauffeur-driven cars, others walked from the bus stop half a mile down the road. On school grounds, social class was expressed in myriad ways, among them fashion, hairstyles, musical taste, hobbies, or the use of French. My situation was perhaps unusual: I passed. On the one hand, my father was a low-ranking employee at the water and power department, and my mother was a homemaker with no income of her own. I felt keenly the stress of living paycheck to paycheck and the continual worry about how much everything cost. On the other hand, my parents had sent me to Sainte Marguerite, a French grade school, and fluency in that language regularly granted me access to elite groups. *Passing* is a word commonly applied to race, but it seems apt for class as well. The language I used every day—the vocabulary I chose, my command of grammar, and especially my accent—placed me in a social class to which I did not belong, but with which I was intimately familiar. Each summer, for instance, I spent several weeks with my best friend, at her family's beachfront property south of Rabat. I was used to rich people, though I wasn't entirely comfortable around them.

Even within my extended family, I observed different classes. My paternal grandfather had left behind a small estate, which my grandmother managed after his death, using it to help her children with down payments on their homes. My father and older uncles, having come of age in the waning days of the colonial era, hadn't had the opportunity for a university education and as a result lived on limited incomes, but the younger uncles had become doctors and executives. A generation later, the gaps between the families were tangible, and could be seen in details large and small. At a relative's wedding, for example, one of my aunts might wear a silk-and-muslin embroidered caftan cinched with a gold belt, while another might be in an off-the-rack polyester caftan. One uncle might vacation in Europe, while another might go camping.

This is not to say that poor people didn't envy or resent the rich, or that the rich didn't treat the poor with pity or contempt. Far from it. I once witnessed a classmate throw an apple core on the ground, and then call her maid—an underage domestic worker—to come pick it up. But both rich and poor understood that their wealth or lack thereof was at least partly a question of circumstance, which is why the poor were not blamed for their poverty. Our faith culture also played a role, in that it emphasized charity. In Morocco, in other words, poverty was a matter of chance. In the United States, it was treated as a matter of choice.

Whatever choices had brought my neighbors and me to the apartment building on South Westmoreland seemed insignificant on the cold night of January 17, 1994, when tectonic plates shifted fifteen miles away, in the San Fernando Valley. The earthquake lasted under twenty seconds, but as I crouched under the door frame of my closet those seconds felt like an eternity. The sound is what I remember most about the Northridge quake: a rumbling in the distance, and then my bed shaking, glasses shattering, chairs tumbling. After the temblor stopped, I came out of my apartment in the pre-dawn darkness, and found all my neighbors in the courtyard. In that moment, we were all bound by the experience of natural disaster. "Are you all right?" Jean asked me. She was in a nylon nightgown that had holes in it, and was hugging herself, visibly shaking. "We have to turn off the water and gas lines," Robert said, and immediately went looking for a wrench. "Does anybody have an extra flashlight?" someone asked.

Over the next few days, we got into the habit of checking in on one another. A sense of trust emerged from the experience, giving our building a renewed feeling of community. In this country, poverty was tragedy—or at least that was the message I gleaned from magazine stories on the subject, which were often illustrated with black-and-white photographs of somber people sitting around kitchen tables. But those days are as colorful in my memory as any I have had: I was doing research I found intellectually satisfying; I had met someone new and was falling in love; I had made many friends on campus. The range of my emotions did not shrink because I had no money. I still felt joy, anger, sadness—and jealousy. The unit above the front gate had huge, sunny windows, one facing out on the street and one on the courtyard. I imagined that its carpet didn't have fleas, its oven didn't emit smoke, its shower drain wasn't clogged—what luxury that would be! Sometimes, I envied the couple who lived there. One day, coming home from campus, I ran into them. "Did you hear what happened last night?" they asked me. Then they took turns telling me about the drive-by shooting overnight. Gunfire wasn't unusual in our neighborhood, and I had learned to live with the sound of sirens and police helicopters, but this time was different. A stray bullet had gone through the window that faced the street.

I stayed in my apartment until the end of the next summer, when my boyfriend and I became engaged and moved in together. That change made me realize, as James Baldwin put it, how extremely expensive it is to be poor. Between my new research assistantship and my boyfriend's fellowship stipend, our monthly income increased just enough that we could afford a security deposit and first month's rent on a one-bedroom apartment in Torrance. We paid $750 a month for it, less than half of what we had jointly paid before. The new apartment had a washer and dryer, so we saved money on laundry every week. In our new zip code, my car insurance rate was lower. The neighborhood also had better air quality, and within weeks the allergies that had afflicted me for months finally cleared up.

When I gave notice to my landlord that I was moving out, he seemed disappointed. During his final walk-through, he asked what I planned to do about my antique desk. I had gotten it when Bullock's on Wilshire Boulevard closed down, and the company that bought the building and removed its art deco artifacts sold what remained of the office furniture for $20 apiece. Strapped onto the trunk of my car, the desk had made the journey two blocks down to my furnished apartment, where it sat against the wall. "It can stay," I said. A bequest to the next tenant, minus the fleas. I handed the keys to my landlord, and remembered his kindness to me when I had signed the lease. He had taken off his reading glasses, fixed me with his blue eyes, and said, "If you're going to be late on your rent, that's fine. Just tell me ahead of time so I can adjust my books. I want to have good people here. That's what matters to me."

At the time, his offer had seemed incredibly charitable, as did the discount he gave Jean on the rent. But now that I think about those days, I am struck by something that had been invisible to me at the time: he had no black tenants. What were the odds of that, with twenty-eight units located three miles from the USC campus? My landlord's assurances that he wanted *good* people (does anyone want *bad* people?) might have been some code I had failed to interpret. After all, I had lived in this country only a short while and the cultural references were still opaque to me. Or perhaps my landlord's rents were simply out of reach for black tenants in the area. I will never know. It is a fact, however, that class intersects with race and gender in ways that are seldom arbitrary.

. . .

Wealth distribution in the United States is not racially indis-
criminate. According to the Census Bureau, median household
income in 2017 was $61,372, but that number varied widely
by race, with white households earning $68,145 and black
households earning $40,258, a gap that, percentage-wise, has
remained virtually unchanged in the last fifty years. Nor is
wealth distribution gender-neutral. Men working full-time, in
year-round jobs, had median earnings of $52,146, while women
in similar situations earned $41,977. Women make, on aver-
age, 80 cents for every dollar a man makes, and the disparity
grows sharply depending on race, with black women making
65 cents and Hispanic women 58 cents for every dollar a white
man makes.

Because wealth is so unevenly distributed, policies that benefit a particular social class also tend to benefit a particular race.
One of the goals of the Social Security Act, which Franklin
D. Roosevelt signed into law in 1935, was to provide monthly
cash benefits, funded through payroll taxes, for retired workers. Practically speaking, Social Security helped senior citizens,
but also their families: the elderly could live independently,
volunteer in their communities, and provide care for their
grandchildren. But while the legislation applied to commerce
and industry workers, it excluded service workers and farm
laborers, who constituted two-thirds of the black working population. As a result, the benefits of Social Security, and its accru-
ing interest for families over the years, were out of reach for a
significant number of black workers, especially in the South.
(These workers would eventually be covered in succeeding
expansions of the Social Security Act—twenty years later.)

The myriad intersections between class, race, and gender

make it difficult to isolate phenomena that can be attributed exclusively to class, but the history of another government assistance program offers a few illuminating clues. At its inception in 1935, welfare (AFDC) was a relatively small part of the Social Security Act that provided cash assistance to children whose father was deceased, absent, or unable to work; the mother was expected to stay home to care for them. The program was state-administered and largely benefited white widows. Black mothers, who were part of the labor force in greater proportions, were generally excluded. States also had a lot of discretionary power in managing grant levels and eligibility requirements for AFDC, with the result that many of them enforced morality standards by denying benefits to unwed mothers and mothers in "unsuitable homes."

After the Great Migration and the Second World War brought black families onto welfare rolls, eligibility rules became stricter and investigations more intrusive. Welfare offices began to conduct "midnight raids" to determine whether a man was present in the home, with the goal of denying benefits to the mother. Then as now, the largest number of welfare recipients were white people. But in 1965, Daniel Patrick Moynihan, a sociologist who worked for the Johnson administration, issued an eponymous report that pathologized black families as broken, with a high rate of households headed by single women, an outcome that he blamed on government assistance, which discouraged their self-sufficiency. (Recall that welfare offices ruled out payments to mothers who had a "man in the house.") Over the next couple of decades, welfare acquired racial and gender connotations it did not have before, and the trend toward surveillance and criminalization of welfare recipients increased.

The racial connotations of welfare programs place poor

whites, like my old neighbor Jean, in a liminal position. Their whiteness grants them undeniable racial privileges, which flow into economic advantages, like higher loan-approval rates compared with applicants of other races. At the same time, these privileges may be invisible to them if they live in towns or counties that are overwhelmingly white. Furthermore, group privileges do not erase their individual difficulties, nor the sense of being looked down upon by the cultural elite, particularly by rich whites. In my travels across the United States, I've often been startled by the ease with which rich liberals resort to terms like "redneck" or "white trash" to dismiss large swaths of white people in red states. The ambiguous position of poor whites can pit racial solidarity against class solidarity in ways that can be manipulated by elected officials, resulting in policies that hurt all the poor, regardless of background.

Although there is some agreement that more should be done to help the poor become self-sufficient, research has consistently shown that programs benefiting the poor receive different support depending on the racial identity of the beneficiaries. In particular, white support for social welfare programs drops when they believe these programs advance nonwhites. This helps explain why politicians appeal to white voters with coded references to welfare programs, a strategy that has been used by both parties. In July 1992, when Bill Clinton accepted the Democratic nomination for the presidency, he said he was doing it "in the name of those who do the work, pay the taxes, raise the kids and play by the rules—in the name of the hardworking Americans who make up our forgotten middle class." Then he famously promised to "end welfare as we know it." Twenty-five years later, standing on the steps of the Capitol, Donald Trump would proclaim that "the forgotten men and women of our country will be forgotten no more." He, too, promised that "we will get our people off of welfare and back to work." Exactly who is not to be forgotten in these speeches, and who is not entitled to government relief, is neither class- nor race-neutral.

Citizenship is characterized not only by civil or political rights—like equality before the law or the right to suffrage— but also by social rights, like education, healthcare, and safe housing. The British sociologist T. H. Marshall argued in 1950 that social rights are the natural evolution of civil and politi- cal rights because the right to suffrage, for example, is better exercised when a citizen is educated, healthy, and housed. This argument was based on white men's experiences in Great Brit- ain, and didn't account for the struggles of citizens of other races and genders, nor for the challenges faced by the millions who lived in outposts of the British Empire. (For instance, British women had access to national health insurance before they gained the right to vote and British subjects had passports, but not the political rights associated with it.) Nevertheless, the connection that Marshall drew between civil, political, and social rights remains useful and significant.

Although welfare programs in the United States—Social Security, unemployment benefits, Medicare, veterans' benefits, supplemental nutrition assistance—are widely popular, the word *welfare* has slowly acquired cultural associations that it did not have when it was conceived. Nowadays, the language that some politicians use to discuss such programs makes attempts to provide citizens with a basic standard of living seem akin to Stalinist efforts at eliminating free will and individual lib- erty. Even benefits that workers and employers pay for through payroll taxes are referred to, often disparagingly, as "entitlements." Warehouses have been renamed "fulfillment centers" and employees have become "associates" or "contractors."

But what language should we use to talk about the fact that just three Americans—Jeff Bezos, Bill Gates, and Warren Buffett—have more wealth than 160 million others? As individuals, these businessmen ought to have the same rights, liberties, and protections as anybody else; instead, their wealth insures that they have more freedom of expression, more power to influence elections, more opportunity to run for public office than millions of the poorest Americans.

Perhaps that is where progress begins—with new language about class. Perhaps we need to widen our understanding of citizenship rights to include guarantees of a decent minimum wage, healthcare, education, and housing. Sometimes, I wonder what this country might look like if no one had to go bankrupt because of medical costs; no one had to be made homeless because of low wages; and no one had to go into debt to receive an education. I don't think that's a particularly radical thing to imagine.

Since moving out of the apartment on South Westmoreland, I have been back in the neighborhood only a handful of times. Once, it was to have dinner at a Korean restaurant that a friend had recommended for its spicy tofu stew. Another time, it was to take part in a rally in support of young undocumented immigrants, which started out at Lafayette Park. On the way to the march, I stopped by my old building. It had been repainted a cheerful blue, and flowering magnolia trees had been planted around the main gate, signals that the area was starting to gentrify. A notice outside said "No Vacancy."

Inheritance

On the day when Christine Blasey Ford testified before the Senate Judiciary Committee that Brett Kavanaugh had attempted to rape her thirty-six years earlier, I was in a hotel room in Hickory, North Carolina. I was scheduled to speak to college students in town about one of my novels, but instead of preparing for my talk I was trying to fix the phone jack. The line was dead, and I couldn't order food. As a matter of fact, I wasn't hungry; I was merely trying to distract myself from the television, where Ford was telling the assembled senators about the summer day in 1982 when Kavanaugh allegedly pinned her down on a bed at a friend's house, tried to remove her clothes, and covered her mouth when she tried to scream. Eventually, I turned off the set and took a two-mile walk to the nearest restaurant, where I ordered breakfast and did my best to ignore the question that many talking heads were still asking that morning: *Why didn't she report him sooner?*

The question was also asked of dozens of actresses who were cast, or hoped to be cast, in Harvey Weinstein's movies over the span of thirty years. It was asked of playwrights who studied under Israel Horovitz, talk-show staff who worked for Charlie Rose and Tavis Smiley, and models who were photographed by Patrick Demarchelier. It was asked of massage therapists at Steve Wynn's casinos in Las Vegas, staff at Mario Batali's restaurants in New York, and fans who met Tariq Ramadan at scholarly conferences in Switzerland. It was asked of nearly every woman who, encouraged by Tarana Burke's Me Too movement, spoke out against sexual harassment and assault that year. It was also asked of Anita Hill, back in 1991, when Clarence Thomas was facing his own confirmation hearings before the Senate Judiciary Committee. *Why didn't she report him sooner?* is a question that comes in different guises. *Why didn't she say no? Why didn't she just leave? Why didn't she tell anyone about it?*

These are questions that I was once young enough and naïve enough to ask with complete sincerity. Twenty-three years ago, after I applied for permanent residency in the United States, submitted to background checks, and paid the required fees, I received a work-authorization card in the mail. The timing was auspicious: I was nearly finished writing my dissertation and felt ready to explore options outside academia. Looking through the job postings in the *Daily Trojan* one morning, I noticed an ad for an editorial position at Channel One News in Los Angeles. I interviewed for it and was hired on the spot. This outcome seemed to me nothing short of miraculous. Maybe the slogan I kept hearing was true—America really was the land of opportunity.

Channel One produced a daily news program, in those days anchored by Anderson Cooper, which was broadcast to thousands of middle and high schools across the U.S., as well as a monthly publication for educators. As deputy editor of this magazine, my job was to write features, edit a few of the other pieces, and generally help with the production. My boss was smart and generous with his time, and my co-workers were friendly and energetic. Our office was on the top floor of

Raleigh Studios, across from Paramount Pictures, where my husband had landed a position in the IT department a couple of years earlier, so I could carpool to work with him if I wanted. In many ways, this job was ideal.

There was one problem, however. On our floor was a television producer who was in the habit of visiting the magazine office unannounced, asking for updates from different staff members, and then giving the women unsolicited hugs. The hugging was couched as part of a gregarious personality: he was always telling jokes or reporting on some adventure he'd had with his friends at bars or restaurants. He seemed particularly fond of a young assistant who sat ten feet from me, a slim brunette whose hair was streaked with blond highlights. She had graduated from college the summer before and was desperate to work in TV. The producer was loud. His voice thundered whether he was happy or angry, and I remember that the assistant would jump to her feet to fetch whatever it was he demanded. Then, presumably by way of thanking her, he would give her a big hug. *Why doesn't she report him?* I wondered.

Whether my co-workers on the floor wondered the same thing, I didn't know. But I did notice that whenever the producer engaged in this behavior, people would exchange embarrassed looks. No one said anything. No one did anything. Two months passed. One morning, I was in the kitchen getting coffee when the young assistant walked in. We talked idly about our weekend plans; she asked if I'd seen a recent blockbuster, whether it lived up to the hype. Then the producer came in, a mug with the logo of the company in his hand. "How's it going, sweetheart?" he asked her.

The young assistant looked uncomfortable. She glanced at me, as if to ascertain whether I had heard the word *sweetheart,* too. But instead of challenging him, she replied to his question with another: "How are you?"

"I'm fantastic," he said, taking the pot of coffee and filling his mug. "How about you?" he asked, now turning to me.

"I'm fine." I was about to leave, but he leaned against the counter, seemingly eager to continue the conversation. I felt I had to engage in polite chatter; he was my boss's boss, after all. When he asked if I liked working at Channel One, whether everything was going well so far, I said everything was great.

"Well," he said, "we're all glad to have you here." Then he tried to hug me.

I stepped to the side, well out of his reach. "Thanks," I said curtly and, because the protective feeling I had toward the young assistant was still warm inside me, I added, "And please don't call her sweetheart." He seemed a little surprised, but didn't say anything.

That was a Friday. On Monday, when I came into the office, I noticed that my boss didn't call an editorial meeting. I asked if he wanted to discuss illustrations for our cover story, but he said we would talk about it later, he needed to finish something else first. At lunch, the entire magazine staff, including the young assistant, stepped out. Something was in the air, but I couldn't quite put my finger on it. I was eating a sandwich at my desk when my boss came over to say he was sorry, but he had to let me go.

I was dumbfounded. Just a week earlier, he had complimented my work on the magazine and specifically praised me for my attention to detail. "Why?" I blurted out.

"My budget is too tight," he said. His gaze kept shifting; he wouldn't look me in the eye. "It's my fault, I'm sorry. I should have considered my budget before I hired you."

Admittedly I had been on staff for only two months, but

never once had the issue of budget come up before. Now my boss didn't even want me to finish the week; he wanted me to clean out my desk and leave. I walked out of the building into the sunshine, feeling dizzy from the swift and unexpected turn the day had taken. It took me a few minutes of gentle puzzling to figure out that my boss didn't want me out. It was the producer who did.

I had been told that the Human Resources department should be a point of contact in case of conflict, but it didn't take me long to realize how the situation that led to my being laid off would be perceived from their end. How could I say definitively whether the magazine had the necessary budget for a particular position? And how could I prove that the confrontation with my boss's boss in the kitchen on Friday morning was the reason I had been laid off on Monday morning? Seeking redress through Human Resources would have required having concrete and incontrovertible evidence, which I couldn't have collected because I hadn't been looking for it. I had no pictures, no emails, no recorded calls to prove what I had witnessed. The process was also flawed because Human Resources departments aren't independent observers; they serve the company, whose interests might be at odds with those of the individual filing the complaint. In the end, all I had accomplished by breaking the silence was losing my job.

Why doesn't she report him?

Because she could lose her livelihood was the immediate answer.

That day in September, when Christine Blasey Ford testified under oath before the Senate Judiciary Committee, she read from a prepared statement, which had been made available to the press beforehand. During a party at a friend's house in 1982, she said, after Brett Kavanaugh allegedly wrestled her onto a bed, "it was hard for me to breathe, and I thought that [he] was going to accidentally kill me." She remained calm as she spoke about the attack and, when questioned about specific details, relied on her expertise as a professor of psychology to explain how memories of traumatic events were locked in the brain. "Indelible in the hippocampus," she said, "is the laughter." The drunken laughter of Brett Kavanaugh and his friend Mark Judge, she said, was the single strongest memory she had of the attack: "They [were] having fun at my expense." In addition to facing the assembled senators, she also had to answer questions from a sex-crimes prosecutor hired by the Republicans on the committee, which gave the proceedings the aura of a trial. The television in the café where I was eating breakfast was turned to the live feed from the Senate, and several people were watching, including the restaurant staff. There was no escape from the story of attempted rape, or from the triggering effect it had on the women who watched it. Afterward, I returned to my hotel room, feeling upset by what I had heard, yet inspired by the bravery of a woman who insisted on telling her story.

By lunchtime, many Republicans who supported Kavanaugh's nomination to the Supreme Court had begun to concede that Dr. Ford's testimony was credible. But now they brought forth a different argument: although she had been attacked, they said, she was confused about the identity of her attacker, who could not have been Judge Kavanaugh. A week before the Senate hearing, Ed Whelan—a former clerk for Antonin Scalia and the president of a conservative think tank committed to "applying the Judeo-Christian moral tradition to critical issues of public policy"—posted a long thread on social media claiming that Ford had been assaulted by a classmate of

Kavanaugh's, whom he named. As evidence for this theory, he used a publicly available floor map of a home where he thought the party might have taken place in 1982 as well as pictures of Kavanaugh and the classmate, showing their supposed physical resemblance. Although Whelan apologized for the conspiracy theory the next day, his strategy was adopted by others in conservative circles. Hours before Christine Blasey Ford's testimony to the Senate, Republicans on the Judiciary Committee announced they had interviewed two men who said that they, and not Kavanaugh, had been the assaulters.

The Democrats on the committee asked Dr. Ford to respond to this new allegation. "With what degree of certainty do you believe Judge Kavanaugh assaulted you?" Dick Durbin asked. "One hundred percent," she replied. "So what you are telling us," Dianne Feinstein said, "is this could not be a case of mistaken identity." "Absolutely not," was the response. What the Senate heard that morning was a woman's story of sexual abuse and its lasting psychological consequences on her, followed by claims of false accusation and mistaken identity made by the accuser's defenders on the very committee charged with scrutinizing the man's record. In the end, the Republican majority decided that Dr. Ford was an unreliable narrator of her own story.

This is a very old trope about the value of a woman's word, and it can be traced back all the way to foundational texts. The British classicist Mary Beard has written extensively about how silencing women is a rite of passage for men: in *The Odyssey*, for example, the teenaged Telemachus tells Penelope to "go in and do your work. Stick to the loom and the distaff. . . . It is for men to talk, especially me. I am the master." Under Athenian law, women could not be litigants, and if they had cases to put forward they were to be represented by men. Jewish law mandates that only men can serve as witnesses in court: "The oath of testimony applies to men, but not to women." Although women were among the earliest followers of Jesus, the apostle Paul counseled that "women should remain silent in the churches. They are not allowed to speak, but must be in submission." And the Qur'an advises that in case of legal conflict, two men should be brought as witnesses, but "if there are not two men [available], then a man and two women from those whom you accept as witnesses—so that if one of the women errs, then the other can remind her." These foundational texts contain the earliest and most influential stories we hear, the inheritance we receive and pass down.

Stories, whether religious or secular, are the primary means by which we interpret the world around us: they help us understand our experiences, draw insight from them, and remember them in order to pass them on to others. Stories about men are so pervasive in popular culture that they seem familiar and valuable, whereas stories about women appear far-fetched and worthless. This observation is borne out by empirical evidence: surveys consistently show that the overwhelming majority of top-grossing Hollywood movies feature men as sole protagonists. Research has also established that there are far more speaking parts for men than women in commercially successful movies.

Exposure to biased portrayals like these feeds certain beliefs about the roles that men and women should play in society. Men act, women submit. Men speak, women listen. Over the course of my professional life, I have sat in dozens of meetings where a note-taker was needed, and the task was immediately delegated to a woman or—and this always filled me with embarrassment for her—she volunteered to do it. Silence is taken to be the natural condition of women, which is why women who speak clearly and forcefully are often attacked as arrogant or aggressive, when they're not labeled fools or liars. When a woman, a citizen of the republic, raises her voice against a man who is being considered for a position as a chief interpreter of the laws of that republic, she is met by senators who tell her that she must be mistaken. Ultimately, this is where the imbalance of the stories we grow up reading, hearing, or watching leads us: a man's story is seen as inherently more authentic than a woman's story. It is disbelief that undergirds the question: *Why didn't she report him sooner?*

Like Christine Blasey Ford, I was born in the suburbs of a capital city. Like her, I have a doctoral degree from the University of Southern California. We graduated a year apart, a fact I discovered after I began writing this chapter. Because her research was focused on experimental psychology and mine on psycholinguistics, it is likely that we took one or more classes together. Was she the young woman who sat behind me in Dr. Cliff's statistics class in Seeley G. Mudd? Or the one who received the summer research assistantship we were all coveting at the end of our first year? Dr. Ford and I had very different upbringings, however. One of the more salient differences for the purposes of this story is that I grew up in an undemocratic country, where the relationship between the state and the individual was as fraught with power as the relationship between the sexes.

When I was a little girl, my mother didn't treat me much differently from my brother: we were expected to go to school, do our homework, clear the table. But this changed when I was about eleven or twelve. Suddenly I was expected to do domestic chores, like washing dishes or mopping floors or scrubbing toilets. When I protested that my brother, older than me by four years, never had to do these tasks, my mother would say, "Your brother runs errands and does yard work." Boys and girls were not the same: chores outside the home were for boys, chores inside the home were for girls. I complained about these differences bitterly and ceaselessly, but my grievances were usually met with a shrug. Boys and girls were not the same.

The sheer repetition of this proposition did not sanctify it in my mind, but it did have the effect of exhausting my protests. By the end of middle school, the future I was being prepared for became clear to me: I had to go to college, find a decent job, and eventually get married and start a family. It was to prepare me for the bliss of domestic life that one day my mother tried to teach me how to cook. "No," I said. This went on for several days, until my mother gave up. "What will you do when you get married?" she lamented. This was not said out of meanness, but out of concern. My mother had not known how to cook when she got married, so she wanted to spare me the difficult experience of being instructed by a demanding mother-in-law, as she had been.

My father didn't get involved in assigning chores, but he exerted his influence in different ways. He allowed my brother to stay out late with his friends, whereas I was expected home before the muezzin called out the sunset prayer. I wasn't allowed to date, of course, and I couldn't spend time with a boy who wasn't a friend of the family or a classmate at my school. Although my father was a secular man, he still thought of his honor as bound up with his daughter's virginity and he wanted to make sure he could protect it. By word and by example, my parents were reinforcing the ambient patriarchal order.

School took care of the rest. In history class, we studied dynasty after dynasty of men who ruled over Morocco, but women who might have played a political role in shaping the nation went largely unmentioned. In biology class, we learned the basics of human reproduction, but skipped over sexual education. In religion class, we were told that men had rights over women; that women should dress modestly and submit to their husbands; and that men were financially responsible for their wives and children. In Arabic and French classes, we read novel after novel in which the main character was a man who faced, and triumphed over, various trials and obstacles.

It seems to me now that the imbalance in literature courses was perhaps the most harmful. We were trained, all of us, to feel more empathy for male heroes, to see the world through their eyes, to feel their pain, their joy, their hopes. We developed an affinity for male taste and male pleasure. We learned to have compassion for men's faults and men's failures. But rarely did we do the same for women protagonists. Is it any wonder, then, that when a man is accused of sexual abuse or assault, so many of us begin with a defensive question: *Why didn't she report him sooner?*

Learning to ask different questions is a lifelong process that, for me, started when I was exposed to the work of Moroccan feminists. I had the great fortune of growing up in a house full of books. My parents were always reading, and so were all of us children. In addition, nothing we read was ever censored or taken away from us. I can see now that all the freedom I didn't have in life, I could find in books. One summer, when I was in high school, my sister pressed into my hands a volume she had just finished reading: *Beyond the Veil* by Fatima Mernissi. This was how I came across a critique of the patriarchal dynamics in our society, rooted in an analysis of Qur'anic texts and their applications to law. In many cases, Mernissi argued, biased interpretations of sacred texts were reified by male scholars, because such interpretations placed or maintained political power in the hands of men. I began to keep up with the work of Mernissi through a column she wrote regularly for the magazine *Femmes du Maroc*.

I think I was searching, dimly, for women who had broken the molds set for them by others. I remember the awe I felt when I watched a television interview with Bouchra Bernoussi when she became the first woman, along with Oumaima Sayeh, to fly commercial airliners for Royal Air Maroc in 1986. The male reporter sat with Bernoussi in the cockpit, asking about her training, her work, her schedule, then closed the interview by posing this question: "If you were given the choice between a bride's gown or a pilot's uniform, which would you choose?" There was apparently some contradiction in his mind between being a pilot and being a wife and mother, and it was clear which direction he would have suggested for her.

Without a moment's hesitation, Bernoussi replied, "A pilot's uniform."

My father, who was watching the interview with me, said: "Well, she's wrong about that."

I was stunned. How could he—a man who always pushed me to excel and succeed—think that a woman's gifts should be subordinated to her husband? "No," I said, turning to him, "she's *not* wrong."

My father tilted his head and, perhaps realizing he was about to get into a long argument with a stubborn teenager, picked up a magazine instead and started reading. I was still fuming at what the interviewer had asked and took no notice of the fact that I had ended the debate.

Years passed, during which I finished high school and went

to college. My education in feminism continued in haphazard ways, guided more by random encounters in the books I read than by any conscious choice I made. One summer, freshly graduated with a degree in linguistics from the University of London, I found a job as a staff writer for a progressive newspaper in Casablanca. This was the sort of publication that would run daily reports about workers' rights, but without ever extending those rights to its own employees, who were not unionized and whose salaries were well below those of staffers at centrist or conservative newspapers. I didn't have the nerve to mind: I had the rare opportunity to write about books, culture, and politics in Rabat, my hometown. I spent my time crisscrossing the city, going from publication parties to art vernissages to press conferences.

One afternoon, I went into the office to meet with my editor. His window was open, and the hum of traffic served as a soundtrack to our conversation. Two other men came in while we spoke, one of them a sportswriter and the other a famous columnist. I can't recall what our conversation was about, though the mood was jovial. When I got up to leave, the famous columnist asked me whether the rumor he'd heard was true, that I had applied to graduate schools and might be going to the United States in the fall. "Yes," I said, with a glance at my editor, with whom I had shared the news just the day before. It surprised me how quickly word had spread around the office.

"Why leave?" the columnist asked me. Peering at me over the rim of his glasses, he said it would be a loss for the newspaper, that I should reconsider. "Keep your job, and do your Ph.D. here. I can be your adviser."

He was a professor of linguistics at the university; his research focus was dialectology. I had no interest in that particular field, and told him as much. "But it's nice of you to offer," I added.

"Maybe you'll change your mind," he said, grabbing my wrist.

"I won't."

"Sit on my lap for a minute."

"What? No!"

"Come on, just for a minute. Sit on my lap."

"No," I said again, and pulled my wrist out of his grip. The sportswriter and the editor laughed. The entire exchange had taken no more than a few seconds, but I was overcome by a mix of emotions: shock at the unexpected turn that the encounter had taken; horror that a man I had admired from afar for many years could do such a thing; and disgust that the other two men present laughed about it.

I left the office and took the train back to Rabat, but didn't tell anyone about what happened. Sexual harassment was so prevalent in Morocco that complaining about it was like complaining about the weather. Even if I had spoken about the incident, I was certain I would not be believed. *Maybe you misunderstood.* And even if I were believed, I would be the one blamed, not him. *What were you wearing?* The episode remains indelible in my mind only because it happened in the workplace, which was new for me. But the experience of sexual harassment itself was nothing new.

I came into my own as a woman when I was made conscious of my body. My mother taught me to cross my legs every time I sat down. If my skirt was short or my shirt tight, I was immediately made aware of the fact. I was twelve the first time a man's eyes lingered over my breasts; thirteen the first time a man groped me on a crowded bus; and sixteen the first time a man followed me on the street. From the time I reached puberty, I was catcalled, fondled, harassed, or threatened in one public place or another. In every man I came across, I feared a predator. Sometimes, he revealed himself in the strangest of places. The tennis instructor who pressed his erection against me while he was showing me how to do a backhand. The urologist who was treating me for a kidney stone and instead gave me a pelvic exam, using his fingers instead of a speculum. The bicyclist who, without breaking his pace as he drove past me, reached out and squeezed my left breast.

I never reported an incident of abuse to the police. In Morocco, people are subjects of the king, not citizens of a state that is accountable to them. The job of the police wasn't to protect the population, but to serve the king and his notables—the Makhzen. During this period of time, which came to be known as the Years of Lead, reports of torture and disappearance of protesters and dissidents at the hands of police were common. No one invited law-enforcement officers into their lives if they could help it. Unless the attack was too violent or too public to ignore, everyone—harasser, harassed, and bystander alike— pretended not to notice the sexual abuse in plain view.

The legal silence was matched by cultural silence. I remember how the sociologist Soumaya Naamane Guessous was greeted on national television when she was promoting *Au-delà de toute pudeur,* a nonfiction book adapted from her doctoral thesis on shame and sexuality in Morocco. The interviewer bluntly asked her whether she intended to attack fundamental values of our society and religion. Without losing her cool, Guessous replied that people should evaluate traditions individually, rather than pass them on to their children wholesale, and that some traditions deserved to be set aside. In a testament to the need for the dialogue that Guessous started, the book became an instant bestseller and a mainstay of college curricula.

Nevertheless, the reality for me, as I'm certain it was for most women of my generation, was a daily confrontation with sexism, sexual harassment, and sexual abuse. Women were not equal to men under the law in Morocco. In those days, the Mudawana (or family code) considered them to be minors, legal and financial responsibility for whom lay in the hands of fathers or husbands. Women couldn't marry without the approval of a guardian; couldn't divorce without cause; couldn't marry a second, third, or fourth spouse; and couldn't inherit the same share as their brothers. If a woman married a foreigner, she could not pass on her citizenship to her children. In fact, though this rule was rarely enforced, a woman couldn't leave the country without the approval of her husband. The relationship between men and women depended entirely on the benevolence of the former and the obedience of the latter, a dynamic that mirrored the relationship between the king and his subjects. In that sense, women were not even subjects; they were second-class subjects. So when they spoke up, they faced denials, disbelief, and outright threats. Yet they continued to speak, forcefully and for many years, in order to change the family code, which was finally reformed in 2004.

Years later, when I wrote a post online about the incident with the columnist, a reader cast doubt on my account, said I was nothing but a striver, and that I was trying to tarnish the impeccable reputation of the man—even though I hadn't named him. Then the reader ended his rant with *Why didn't she report him sooner?*

Because she would get responses like this was another answer.

. . .

That day in September, when Brett Kavanaugh's turn came to testify before the Senate Judiciary Committee, he told a markedly different story, and in a markedly different tone. By turns teary and angry, he said that he was wholly innocent of the accusation against him, which had caused his family to be "totally and permanently destroyed," and called the hearing "a circus." He submitted to the committee a calendar from 1982 that showed he was out of town "almost every weekend," treating it as irrefutable proof that he could not have attended an impromptu party with Christine Blasey Ford on a weekday. Although he did not mention his friend Mark Judge by name, he insisted there were no corroborating witnesses to the alleged assault, and called the accusations against him "an orchestrated political hit." When he was asked by Democratic senators whether he would support an FBI investigation, he repeatedly refused to answer the question, saying instead that he would abide by the committee's decision. It was difficult to get him to speak on the record about his past drinking excesses or even to get him to say how much drinking was too much. For example, when Amy Klobuchar asked him whether he had ever had blackouts from drinking, he shot back "Have you?"

The contrast between Judge Kavanaugh and Dr. Ford was startling. The man was emotional and uncooperative, luxuries the woman could not afford if she wanted her story to be believed. As the hearing continued into the late afternoon, the judge's behavior became increasingly testy. Watching his testimony from my hotel room in North Carolina, I felt he had done irreparable harm to his candidacy. Perhaps Lindsey Graham, the senior senator from South Carolina, felt this, too, because when his turn came to speak, he delivered an angry rebuke of the entire process. "What you want to do," he yelled at his Democratic colleagues on the committee, his face turning pink from his exertions, "is to destroy this guy's life [and] hold this seat open."

For Graham, the allegations against Kavanaugh were not true—*could not be true*—because he was nominated by a Republican president and would shift the balance of the Supreme Court rightward for a generation. Graham perceived the case as a wholly partisan attempt by Democrats to hold on to a Supreme Court seat, and could not conceive of it any other way. Speaking to the press earlier that day, he said he did not believe that Ford's allegations would justify even "a search warrant or an arrest warrant." This is why he did not use his allotted time to ask about the allegations, but instead to lecture the committee and the public about the irreparable harm that had been done to an innocent man.

But the most telling moment for me came when Senator Kamala Harris asked Brett Kavanaugh, "Did you watch Dr. Ford's testimony?" "I did not," he replied. The Republican members of the committee had already decided that Dr. Ford was an unreliable narrator of her story. Judge Kavanaugh, on the other hand, had decided that her story wasn't even worth hearing.

Why didn't she report him sooner? In fact, she had. Six years before the Judiciary Committee hearing, Dr. Ford had told her couples' therapist about being assaulted by a boy at "an elitist prep school" in the Washington, D.C., area and the lasting trauma she had suffered as a result. It was only when she found out that Brett Kavanaugh had been nominated to the Supreme Court that she wrote to her senator in California—

Dianne Feinstein—to share her concerns. Kavanaugh was being considered for a lifetime seat on the highest court in the land, a position from which he would be able to decide federal cases, including cases of assault and rape. It was her civic duty, she said, to report what she knew about the man. "My original intent was first and foremost to be a helpful citizen," she said.

Although she tried to keep her story confidential, it was leaked, allegedly by a friend, to Ryan Grim of *The Intercept*. This left Ford with no option but to speak publicly about her experience. What happens when a citizen of the female persuasion comes forward with allegations against a man who is being considered for a position as a justice of the state? Dr. Ford was immediately flooded with death threats. She was forced to hire private security guards, at her own expense, and to move with her husband and children four times. For several months, as threats against her continued, she could not return to her job at Palo Alto University. But Judge Kavanaugh was sworn in nine days after her testimony.

It took a little longer—twelve days—for Clarence Thomas to be sworn in after Anita Hill testified that he had sexually harassed her when she worked for him at the Department of Education and later at the Equal Employment Opportunity Commission. Over the course of two years, she said, he had repeatedly asked her out on dates, mentioned his sexual prowess, and talked in graphic detail about pornographic movies he had seen. Like Dr. Ford, Professor Hill made a private allegation of harassment, in this case to an FBI agent who was investigating the nominee prior to Senate confirmation, but the report was leaked to NPR's Nina Totenberg. Like Dr. Ford, Anita Hill had to testify in public about what had happened years earlier and did so in a candid and composed manner. Once, she said, while they were alone in his office at the EEOC,

Clarence Thomas had asked her "Who put pubic hair in my Coke?" Another time, she said, while he was discussing the adult movies he enjoyed watching, he described a male star as "Long Dong Silver." Though it was difficult to recount these workplace encounters in a national, televised forum, she felt she had to tell the truth. "I could not keep silent," she said.

Breaking the silence is a woman's greatest offense, and the culture swiftly punishes her for it. Like Dr. Ford, Professor Hill was treated as an unreliable narrator of her own story. Senator Heflin of Alabama, a Democrat, asked if she was "a scorned woman," if she had a "militant attitude relative to civil rights," what she knew about "fantasy" or "fantasies," and if she was writing a book—meaning, I suppose, a book that would make her rich and famous. All these insinuations she denied. Senator Hatch of Utah, a Republican, suggested that she had gotten the idea for the pubic hair allegation from the novel *The Exorcist,* and that she found inspiration for the "Long Dong Silver" anecdote from *Carter v. Sedgwick County*, a 1988 legal case that had been decided by the Tenth Circuit Court of Appeals, which, he was sure, was available at law schools in the state of Oklahoma, where Anita Hill taught. This is what a female citizen must be prepared for if she brings allegations against a male justice of the state: she will be treated as deranged.

Of course, Professor Hill was asked why she hadn't reported the sexual harassment immediately; why she had followed Clarence Thomas from the DoE to the EEOC; and why she had remained in touch with him after she left government for academia. She explained that, at the time, the Reagan administration was trying to shutter the DoE and she had no job prospects, particularly in civil rights, her area of interest; that the sexual harassment had waned in the weeks leading to the offer of a position at the EEOC; and that she needed a reference from her former employer after she landed a position as a law professor at Oral Roberts University. Although her allegation was corroborated by a friend of hers—Susan Hoerchner, then a workers' compensation judge in California, who testified that Hill had spoken contemporaneously about the sexual harassment she endured in the workplace—the tone of questioning by the fourteen senators, all of whom were men, was frequently hostile. Joe Biden, who chaired the proceedings, was particularly unsympathetic. He did not call on three other female witnesses who were prepared to corroborate the allegations, and allowed Clarence Thomas to testify twice, once before and once after Anita Hill.

All of the committee members were white, as well, a fact that Judge Thomas pointed out during the second part of his testimony, which was broadcast in prime time. He felt himself to be a victim, and said that, from his standpoint as a black American, "it is a high-tech lynching for uppity-blacks who in any way deign to think for themselves, to do for themselves, to have different ideas, and it is a message that, unless you kowtow to an old order, this is what will happen to you, you will be lynched, destroyed, caricatured by a committee of the U.S. Senate, rather than hung from a tree." In Clarence Thomas's estimation, it was racism alone that drove members of the committee to dignify the private allegations against him with a public hearing, a charge that pitted viewers' gender and race allegiances against each other. In this framing, to side with Anita Hill was to side with feminists—but also with racists.

In all other respects, Judge Thomas's testimony was remarkably similar to Judge Kavanaugh's. He, too, denied the accusations completely and forcefully. He, too, said that his reputation had been irreparably harmed, telling the senators that "there is nothing this committee, this body, or this country can do to give me my good name back, nothing." He, too, offered up his past record for scrutiny, pointing out that he had worked with hundreds of women and that none, other than Anita Hill, had ever made public allegations of sexual harassment. He, too, called the proceedings "a circus." And he, too, refused to listen to the woman who testified against him. When asked whether he had heard Anita Hill speak, he replied, "No, I didn't. I've heard enough lies."

Once I was a subject in a monarchy; now I'm a citizen in a republic. The immigration experience has shown me how membership in a nation-state is gendered in a variety of ways: in neither country have I felt that I had the same rights as a man, the same responsibilities, the same status, or the same opportunities. Class, race, and ethnicity are additional modalities that I need to include here, because they further complicate that relationship. In the United States, white women have fared better at every step of the struggle for equality than nonwhite women. In Morocco, those modalities are just as much in effect. For example, abortion remains illegal except in medical emergencies, but Moroccan women who can afford the procedure routinely have it, making the issue of abortion a class problem as much as a legal one.

I have not felt fully free or fully equal in either country. When a friend of mine, a lawyer by profession, heard me say that I didn't feel I had the same status as a man in the United States, he responded with an incredulous *"Really?"* I think what he left unsaid is that, having been born and raised in Morocco, I ought to feel grateful to live in America, where women's rights are presumably more advanced. This attitude is also common among opinion writers across much of the political spectrum.

The *real* war on women, I'm periodically informed, is *over there*: female genital mutilation in Egypt, Sudan, or Somalia; gender segregation and forced veiling in Iran and Saudi Arabia; child marriage and illiteracy in Afghanistan; bride kidnapping in Chechnya and Kyrgyzstan; sex-selective abortion in China and India; or femicide in Mexico and El Salvador, to name just a few of the offenses against women that come readily to mind.

It's a facile argument, but I fear it's also insidious. Suggesting that women who live in democratic countries should be grateful for the rights they have subtly discourages these same women from trying to reach full equality with men. Although American women make up half of the electorate, they have yet to reach parity in political power: only 23 percent of elected representatives in the 116th Congress are women—and that's a record. Women in this country make less money for the same work, and the disparity in salary varies widely by race and ethnicity. Child marriage, so frowned upon *over there*, is legal in forty-eight states, and in the vast majority of these unions, the child is a girl. The list goes on.

At the moment, abortion is still legal in the U.S., but access to clinics for the procedure has been so constrained over the last thirty years as to make it unavailable for many women. The states of Wyoming, North Dakota, and South Dakota are down to one clinic each, for example. After Brett Kavanaugh was sworn onto the Supreme Court, several state legislatures (Missouri, Alabama, Georgia, Ohio, Mississippi) moved to outlaw abortion at six weeks of pregnancy, making the procedure virtually impossible to get, and forcing legal challenges that will likely go to the Supreme Court. It is entirely possible that, in the near future, an alleged rapist will have a deciding vote on whether a rapist can force his victim to keep the fetus with which he has impregnated her.

What I want is freedom, not better conditions of subjugation. Every day, when I step outside of my home, a certain part of my mind is immediately occupied with keeping myself safe: I'm aware of how the clothes I happen to have reached for that morning look on my body; how this body, clothed in this particular way, might be perceived by strangers in public; whether the small talk I'm making as I wait on the coffee line might be perceived as flirting; how close a man walking behind me on the street is to me; whether it is safe to leave my office door unlocked at this or that time; whether it's too late or too dark to cross the parking lot alone. It is a constant surveillance of the self for the sake of being safe from violence, and for the sake of not being asked, in case the violence against my body should happen, *Why didn't she report him sooner?*

Do Not Despair of This Country

"All men are created equal," Thomas Jefferson wrote in 1776, while he kept 135 men, women, and children as slaves on his plantation at Monticello. This is a contradiction that he somehow accommodated, just as many people do today when they claim that everyone is equal yet promote or support policies that ensure systemic and enduring inequality in this country. American citizenship, which ought to grant the same rights to all who hold it, has been historically circumscribed by a number of conditions that are almost entirely determined by the lottery of birth. In this book, I have written about a few of these conditions—race, gender, faith, and national origin. But there are others—ability, gender expression, and sexual orientation, to name just a few that come readily to mind. Each of these conditions affects interactions between the state and the citizen, whether in the voting booth or at a border checkpoint, during a police encounter or a hospital visit, in decisions about school zoning or government assistance. As a result, the full rights, liberties, and protections of citizenship are still not shared equally by all Americans.

We know what conditional citizenship looks like. It may be useful now to ask what equal citizenship might look like. In a thriving pluralistic democracy, the right to vote is universal, with no restrictions on suffrage that target classes of individuals based on race, class, gender, region, or other markers of identity. Burdens on the vote—voter ID laws, polling station closures, and lengthy residence requirements—are eliminated. All elections allow for early, mail-in, and absentee voting, in order to encourage participation and to reflect the will of all citizens who wish to take part in the plebiscite. Election days are holidays, so that people who cannot afford to take a few hours off from work to stand in the voting line can still take part in the electoral process.

The right to vote is also perennial. The 1.5 million Americans who are currently serving prison sentences and the 6.1 million more who have felony records are no less entitled to electoral representation and no less capable of rational political choice than anyone else. If their incarceration does not revoke their right to work, nor their duty to pay taxes on the minuscule wages they receive, then it should not revoke their right to electoral representation. The termination of voting rights for felons is portrayed, even in some liberal circles, as an ordinary matter of security. But if the prospect of allowing incarcerated or formerly incarcerated people to vote threatens the functioning of a government, one must ask why this government incarcerates so many people as to threaten its existence. The states of Florida, Kentucky, Tennessee, and Virginia, which have some of the most restrictive voting laws in the country, prevent one in five African-Americans from taking part in the electoral process. By contrast, Vermont and Maine—the two whitest states in the Union—already allow inmates to vote, and have suffered no detectable setback to the operation of their democracies. The universal right to suffrage is the most basic element of equal citizenship.

Equal citizens have social rights to education, healthcare,

a living wage, safe drinking water, and clean air. Rights that many people would claim as natural—government by consent, for example—cannot be meaningfully exercised if citizens cannot distinguish between real and fake news; if their healthcare costs have made them homeless; if they cannot afford to go to a polling place; or if climate disasters have exiled them from their hometowns. Without social rights, legal and civil rights in this country are going to be enjoyed by an increasingly smaller group of people, leaving the majority shut out of the wealth that their own labor helps create. Being a part of the American community should guarantee a basic standard of living, which in turn increases the chances of civic participation by all who are eligible.

Equal citizens have ownership of their bodies. We are entitled to physical privacy, sexual consent if we are of legal age and sound mind, and freedom to make medical decisions about pregnancy, abortion, and end-of-life care. The state's interference in issues of bodily integrity should be limited to matters of public health, such as the prevention of communicable diseases or the regulation of pharmaceutical drugs. Perhaps the most challenged of the rights regarding bodily autonomy is the right to abortion, in which the state is assumed by some to be the best representative of the interests of the fetus, regardless of its health, chances of survivability, or manner of conception. But for the state to compel a woman to carry a fetus to term against her wishes is akin to compelling her to donate a part of her body because the state has decided that another, worthier person needs that organ donation to survive. Furthermore, the state does not declare itself a custodian of fertilized embryos outside the womb; it trusts fertility clinics to implant or destroy them depending on viability or medical need. It must therefore also trust women to make medical decisions about their bodies.

Equal citizens have a right to be free of harassment and discrimination, whether by the state or private entities, and, if those freedoms are breached, they can seek redress through state institutions. The legal apparatus that is supposed to provide protection still fails many Americans. For instance, Title VII of the Civil Rights Act, which protects workers from discrimination, applies only to businesses with fifteen or more employees. With millions of people in smaller workplaces, and with the new corporate practice of reclassifying employees as contractors, protection from discrimination is not yet a right guaranteed to all. In addition, the agreements that force many workers into secret arbitration with their employers make it not only more difficult to receive justice, but can also perpetuate patterns of racial or sexual abuse and pay discrimination in the workplace. All workers have a right to a safe workplace.

Equal citizens are free to exercise any or no religion, and are protected from state promotion of, or discrimination against, any religion. For example, the Supreme Court decision in *Trump v. Hawaii,* which allowed the administration to ban immigrants from five Muslim countries, is an egregious violation of the religious neutrality that should apply to the government. In her dissent, Justice Sotomayor wrote that "based on the evidence in the record, a reasonable observer would conclude that the [presidential] Proclamation was motivated by anti-Muslim animus. . . . The majority holds otherwise by ignoring the facts misconstruing our legal precedent, and turning a blind eye to the pain and suffering the Proclamation inflicts upon countless families and individuals, many of whom are United States citizens." The ban must be overturned.

Equal citizens have freedom of movement. They can reside, work, and travel anywhere in the country without profiling or harassment. They are not subjected to roadside checkpoints as a matter of course, nor is their ancestry used to justify a police stop or inspection. Recent advances in technology present new challenges to citizens' privacy and freedom of movement. For instance, many U.S. cities have begun to use license plate readers (LPRs), which are mounted on roadside scanners, patrol cars, or aerial drones, to collect data about drivers. Law-enforcement officers say that LPRs help them to find stolen vehicles or even kidnapped children, but the technology is also used to store data about innocent drivers, their locations, and their habits, in perpetuity. Some workplaces have also begun to integrate LPR technology in parking structures, allowing them to track employee movements during workdays. The surveillance capabilities of many new technologies—face-recognition software, Internet of Things, cell-site simulators—are just beginning to be revealed. As they become more integrated into our lives, we have to ensure that freedom of movement and freedom of association, two of the most basic liberties of citizenship, are still protected.

As I write about equal citizenship, I find myself under the grip of a sudden trepidation, as though the desire for justice were itself fraught with danger. But I must voice this desire, because voicing it is the first step in making it a reality. Undoubtedly, there are many more issues that need to be addressed if we are committed to equality of citizenship. I don't know how many will be met in my lifetime, but as Frederick Douglass once put it, I do not despair of this country.

Despair is seductive. It takes no effort and gives a way out. It says, *Why bother. Look away, there's nothing you can do. Worry about yourself, forget everyone else.* Sometimes, despair swaddles itself in cleverness. Then it speaks as a cynic. *What were you expecting*, it asks with a bitter laugh. *It was ever thus. Plus ça change, right?* Every once in a while, despair betrays itself as fear. *You will lose the fight*, it says. *You will lose time, money, maybe even friends or family*. But despair is never without consequence. It is a gift to the status quo.

There was a lot of despair in the country after the last presidential election. Yet even if the outcome had been different, it would not have replaced the people who make up this nation, nor the systems of inequality and exclusion that many voters support or tolerate. Dismantling these deeply entrenched systems requires radical imagination and lifelong commitment. The task may seem monumental, but there is nothing insurmountable about the struggle for equal citizenship. We live in the country we have today because of choices made by people who came before us, some of whom have been dead for decades, even centuries. We ought to make the kinds of decisions that, decades from now, will result in a better, more equal country.

Sometimes, the difference between stasis and progress is stark and clearly articulated on an election ballot. Other times, it is intentionally muddled by outrageous claims or false advertisements, leaving people confused about which policy or candidate to support. I recall receiving a call the night before the 2008 election, telling me to vote yes on Proposition 8 if I was in support of gay marriage; in fact, I wanted to vote no, since the initiative sought to *ban* same-sex unions that had been recently celebrated in my state. There are also situations where the consequences of a particular political choice are immediate and others where the consequences can take years, perhaps even decades, to unfold. Only by staying engaged can we hope to make informed decisions. Citizenship is made meaningful by the active practice of educating ourselves about how the political, educational, and social choices we make affect others of different races, genders, classes, or backgrounds.

But elections are not enough. Change takes different forms—social activism, legal action, cultural organizing, coalition building, volunteer work. Each has a role to play. I find my greatest inspiration in the people who do the unglamorous labor, day after day, of confronting inequality and exclusion at a local level. I am thinking of the couple I met some years ago, both of them retired lawyers in Florida, who spend their free time providing legal assistance for those in need or the group of mothers I know who organized to open libraries in California schools that didn't have them. If we want change, we must be agents of change.

In any discussion of change, there comes a time to choose partners. In the last few years, many opinion writers have urged dialogue and compromise. Only by talking about differences of opinion, the argument goes, can we hope to reach resolution. Certainly, there are disagreements that can be resolved through debate: the size of the transportation budget, say, or the allocation to Job Corps training programs. But some disagreements are not bridgeable. Separating asylum-seeking children from their parents, for example, is not an issue on which I see a possible compromise. I also believe that, in forming coalitions, we have to think broadly. When American citizens vote in a presidential election, their choices affect people thousands of miles away—in Yemen or Palestine, in Afghanistan or El Salvador. Active citizenship involves an awareness that each decision we make affects others, just as others' decisions in turn affect us.

A few years after my citizenship ceremony, I found myself in our nation's capital for the first time. Naturally, I visited some of the major landmarks: the Washington Monument, the

Lincoln Memorial, the Vietnam War Memorial. But the monument that left the most lasting impression on that first trip was the Jefferson Memorial, which bears these words etched in marble: "Laws and institutions must go hand in hand with the progress of the human mind. As that becomes more developed, more enlightened, as new discoveries are made, new truths discovered and manners and opinions change, with the change of circumstances, institutions must advance also to keep pace with the times." So we must amend his words. All people are created equal—and we must work to make sure that so they remain.

Source Notes

ALLEGIANCE

3 I became an American: "Love and Betrayal in America" by Laila Lalami. *The New Yorker* online. February 3, 2017.

4 Ushers directed us to Building Four: Expo Hall Four—otherwise known as Building Four on correspondence from the Department of Justice—is located inside the Pomona Fairplex.

6 facts that make of me a conditional citizen: "Conditional Citizens" by Laila Lalami. *The Nation*. October 10, 2016.

7 a dynamic that Edward Said described: *Orientalism* by Edward Said. Pantheon Books, 1978.

7 In a comprehensive survey of representation in Hollywood films: *Reel Bad Arabs: How Hollywood Vilifies a People* by Jack Shaheen. Olive Branch Press, 2014.

8 a flyer from the Muslim Public Affairs Council: MPAC's endorsement of George W. Bush was made in concert with several other Muslim American organizations. See, for example, "For Muslim Americans, Influence in Politics Still Hard to Come By" by Dean E. Murphy. *New York Times,* October 27, 2000.

8 As presidential candidate, Bush had courted the Arab and Muslim vote: For details on this strategy, see *What Changed When Everything Changed: 9/11 and the Making of National Identity* by Joseph Margulies. Yale University Press, 2013. See also: "How

the GOP Lost the Arab-American Voters" by Nancy Kaffer. *Politico*. August 3, 2016.

9 He received more than 45,000 votes from various Muslim communities: "America's First Muslim President" by Suhail A. Khan. *Foreign Policy*. August 23, 2010.

9 Bush's claims that he was "a different kind of Republican": "'Armies of Compassion' in Bush's plans" by Dan Balz. *Washington Post*. April 25, 1999. See also: "Bush Campaigns on Issues of a 'Different' Republican" by Katharine Q. Seelye. *New York Times*. June 27, 2000.

13–14 hate crimes against Muslims spiked, accounting for 27 percent of all religious-bias crimes in 2001: Federal Bureau of Investigation. Hate Crime Statistics. 2001.

14 for proclaiming that "the face of terror is not the true faith of Islam": "Bin Laden Is Wanted 'Dead or Alive,' President Says" by David E. Sanger. *New York Times*. September 18, 2001.

14 "Either you are with us or you are with the terrorists": Transcript of George W. Bush's address to Congress. September 20, 2001. White House archives.

14 Advertisers began pulling their support from *Politically Incorrect*: "In Patriotic Time, Dissent Is Muted" by Bill Carter and Felicity Barringer. *New York Times*. September 28, 2001.

14 the "campaign to infantilize the public": "Tuesday, and After." *The New Yorker*. September 24, 2001.

16 "Sir, prove to me that you are not working with our enemies": CNN's Beck to first-ever Muslim congressman: "[W]hat I feel like saying is, 'Sir, prove to me that you are not working with our enemies'" by Rob Dietz. *Media Matters*. November 15, 2006.

17 "Either you are with us," he said later: Transcript of George W. Bush's remarks in Charlotte, North Carolina, at a rally in support of Elizabeth Dole for the Senate. October 24, 2002. White House archives.

18 During a town hall in Lakeville, Minnesota: "McCain: Obama Not an Arab, Crowd Boos" by Jonathan Martin and Amie Parnes. *Politico*. October 10, 2008. "McCain Asks Supporters to

Show Obama Respect" by Laura Meckler. *Wall Street Journal*. October 12, 2008.

19 as many as 25 percent of Americans believed the lie: "A Startling Number of Americans Still Believe President Obama Is a Muslim" by Sarah Pulliam Bailey. *Washington Post*. September 24, 2015.

20 "This is not Dick Cheney we're talking about here": "Obama on Drones: I'm Not Dick Cheney" by Natasha Lennard. *Salon*. March 14, 2013.

21 On the contrary, he called America "foolish": All quotes here are from a compilation made by *Vice News*. "Trump Says If You Don't Love America, Leave It. He's Been Bashing the U.S. for Years" by Ben Craw and Oliver Noble. *Vice News*. July 20, 2019.

21 Rudy Giuliani, the president's lawyer: "Rudy Giuliani Admits It Is a Muslim Ban." YouTube.

21 the State Department issued well over 70,000 visas: The State Department Visa Office Annual Report. FY2008–2017

22 the ban affects millions of Americans: See, for example, "Between War and the Ban: A Yemeni-American Story." *Fault Lines*. Al-Jazeera English. April 25, 2018.

23 treaties that were meant to last "as long as water flows": In his address to the Cherokee who had been removed to Arkansas in 1817, President Monroe told them "you are now in a country where you can be happy; no white man shall ever again disturb you; the Arkansas [River] will protect your southern boundary when you get there. You will be protected on either side; the white shall never again encroach upon you, and you will have a great outlet to the West. As long as water flows, or grass grows upon the earth, or the sun rises to show your pathway, or you kindle your camp fires, so long shall you be protected from your present habitations." See: *Beyond the Frontier: Exploring Indian Country* by Stan Hoig. University of Oklahoma Press, 1998.

23 The proverbial "forty acres and a mule": "The Truth Behind 'Forty Acres and a Mule'" by Henry Louis Gates, Jr. *The African Americans: Many Rivers to Cross*. PBS. 2013.

24 For example, African-Americans: "Breaking Down Mass Incarceration in the 2010 Census: State-by-State Incarceration Rates by Race/Ethnicity" by Leah Sakala. *Prison Policy Initiative.* May 28, 2014.

24 Michelle Alexander showed persuasively: *The New Jim Crow: Mass Incarceration in the Age of Colorblindness* by Michelle Alexander. The New Press, 2010.

24 A black child who becomes involved in a school infraction: "Discipline Disparities for Black Students, Boys, and Students with Disabilities" U.S. Government Accountability Office. April 4, 2018. "What Can Be Done to Stop the Criminalization of Black Girls? Rebuild the System" by Monica Rhor. *USA Today.* May 15, 2019.

25 the Fourth Circuit Court of Appeals: "Voter ID Laws Take a Beating in U.S. Courts" by Michael Wines and Alan Blinder. *New York Times.* July 29, 2016.

25 Conditional citizens are more likely to be expatriated or denaturalized: "Stripping Naturalized Immigrants of Their Citizenship Isn't New" by Kritika Agarwal. *Smithsonian Magazine.* July 24, 2018. See also: "When Saying 'I Do' Meant Giving Up Your U.S. Citizenship" by Meg Hacker. *Prologue Magazine.* National Archives. Spring 2014.

26 In 2002, the New York Police Department: "NYPD: Muslim Spying Led to No Leads, Terror Cases" by Adam Goldman and Matt Apuzzo. Associated Press. August 21, 2012. "New York Drops Unit That Spied on Muslims" by Matt Apuzzo and Joseph Goldstein. *New York Times.* April 15, 2014.

28 But the site once served a different purpose: Pomona (Detention Facility). Densho Encyclopedia, 2019.

28 "Aliens to Go to Pomona": *Los Angeles Times.* May 9, 1942.

28 a brass plaque at the site of internment: "How the Unjust Detention of 5,434 Japanese-Americans at Pomona Fairplex is now memorialized" by Neil Nisperos. *Daily Bulletin.* August 24, 2016.

FAITH

29 In the spring of 2015, I gave a reading from my third novel: "For or Against" by Laila Lalami. *New York Times Magazine.* November 29, 2015.

34 This wave of repression: A lot has been written about the Years of Lead, from political as well as personal perspectives. The following memoirs may be relevant to those who want a first-person account of that period: *Tazmamart, Cellule 10* by Ahmed Marzouki. Tarik Editions, 2000. *Kabazal: Les Emmurés de Tazmamart. Mémoires de Salah et Aïda Hachad* by Abdelhak Serhane. Tarik Editions, 2003. *La Prisonnière* by Malika Oufkir and Michèle Fitoussi. Grasset, 1999. *Oufkir: Un Destin Marocain* by Stephen Smith. Calmann-Lévy, 1999. For an academic analysis, see, for example: "A Truth Commission for Morocco" by Susan Slyomovics. *Middle East Report* 218 (Spring 2001).

34 In middle school, I had known only one girl: For an analysis of the rise of conservatism in women's dress, see *A Quiet Revolution: The Veil's Resurgence from the Middle East to America* by Leila Ahmed. Yale University Press, 2011.

35 The 1997 elections led to two significant developments: "Democratization Without Democracy: Political Openings and Closures in Modern Morocco" by Catherine Sweet. *Middle East Report* 218 (Spring 2001): 22–25. "Rituals of Power and Political Parties in Morocco: Limited Elections as Positional Strategies" by Mohamed Daadaoui. *Middle Eastern Studies* 46, no. 2 (March 2010): 195–21. "Maroc: l'émergence de l'islamisme sur la scène politique" by Khadija Mohsen-Finan. *Politique étrangère* 70, no. 1 (Spring 2005): 73–84.

36 "I reside in this country by reason of great necessity": Omar ibn Said Collection. Library of Congress.

37 A woman baptized Silvia King: Silvia King, Marlin, Texas. Federal Writers' Project: Slave Narrative Project, vol. 16, Texas, part 2, Easter-King. 1936. Library of Congress.

37 Some scholars have also argued: "Phillis Wheatley: A Muslim Connection" by Will Harris. *African American Review* 48, no. V2 (2015): pp. 1–15.

38 In 1929, Syrian and Lebanese: See "North Dakota Mosque a Symbol of Muslims' Long Ties in America" by Samuel G. Freedman. *New York Times.* May 27, 2016.

39 Born in 1966 in the town of Zarqa: "The Short, Violent Life of Abu-Musab al-Zarqawi" by Mary Anne Weaver. *The Atlantic.* July/August 2006. See also "Key Events in the Life of al-Zarqawi." *New York Times.* June 8, 2006.

41 The people of Raqqa had to obey laws: "How ISIS Rules" by Sarah Burke. *New York Review of Books.* February 5, 2015. "Scenes from Daily Life in the De Facto Capital of ISIS" with illustrations by Molly Crabapple. *Vanity Fair.* October 6, 2014.

47 half the people in this country: "Few Would Vote for a Muslim President." *Rasmussen Reports.* September 24, 2015.

BORDERS

48 The Border Patrol agent watched our Prius approach: "Over the Edge" by Laila Lalami. *New York Times Magazine.* April 29, 2017.

49 there are 136 checkpoints just like Sierra Blanca: "Border Patrol Sectors." U.S. Customs and Border Protection website.

49 The *Arizona Republic* estimated that: "Border Patrol Traffic Stops Stir Public Backlash, Site Monitoring" by Bob Ortega. *Arizona Republic.* June 6, 2014.

49 Sierra Blanca is perhaps the most notorious: "The Best Little Checkpoint in Texas" by Al Reinert. *Texas Monthly.* August 2013.

49 the Justice Department gave Border Patrol agents the right to monitor: Background on the Justice Department regulations that allow Border Patrol to set up checkpoints can be found on CBP's website: https://help.cbp.gov/app/answers/detail/a_id/1084/~/legal-authority-for-the-border-patrol. See also: "The

Constitution in the 100-mile Border Zone," factsheet by the ACLU, and "The Long History of America's Constitutionally-Challenged 'Border Zones' " by Jessie Guy-Ryan. *Atlas Obscura.* August 1, 2016.

50 Each year, hundreds of U.S. citizens are wrongfully held in immigration jails: For those who may be curious, two NPR stories provide firsthand accounts: "U.S. Citizen Who Was Held by ICE for 3 Years Denied Compensation by Appeals Court" by Camila Domonoske. *The Two-Way.* NPR. August 1, 2017. See also: "You Say You're an American, But What If You Had to Prove It or Be Deported?" by Eyder Peralta. *The Two-Way.* NPR. December 22, 2016.

51 they were severed from each other when an eighteen-foot-tall fence was erected: "El Paso and Juarez Know What Happens When a Wall Divides Two Cities" by Nigel Duara. *Los Angeles Times.* January 15, 2017.

52 The wall along the southern border is a relatively recent structure: For a history of the wall, see, for example, "The Wall" by Jean Guerrero and Leo Castañeda. *KPBS Midday Edition.* November 13, 2017. "Walled Off" by Laila Lalami. *The Nation.* June 3–10, 2019.

52 the Clinton administration launched Operation Gatekeeper: See *Operation Gatekeeper: The Rise of the "Illegal Alien" and the Remaking of the U.S.-Mexico Boundary* by Joseph Nevins. Routledge, 2002. See also: "New Border Defense Stems Volume of Illegal Crossings" by B. Drummond Ayres, Jr. *New York Times.* October 6, 1994.

52 It was built using helicopter landing pads recycled from the Vietnam War: "The Militarization of the Southern Border Is a Long-Standing American Tradition" by Greg Grandin. *The Nation.* January 14, 2019.

52 "imperial recycling": "Imperial Designs: Remembering Vietnam at the US–Mexico Border Wall" by Victoria Hattam. *Memory Studies* 9, no. 1 (2015): 27–47.

52 "Unfortunately the United States has not been in complete con-

trol": "President Bush Signs Secure Fence Act." October 26, 2006. White House Archives.

53 an increased militarization of the border: "Operation Gatekeeper: An Investigation into Allegations of Fraud and Misconduct." Inspector General's Office Special Report. July 1998. https://oig.justice.gov/special/9807/gkp01.htm.

53 Between 1993 and 2017, the budget of the Border Patrol increased tenfold: "FY2019 Budget Request: U.S. Customs and Border Protection." Center for Migration Studies. 2018. "The Cost of Immigration Enforcement and Border Security." American Immigration Council Report. 2017.

54 "When Mexico sends its people": "Donald Trump's False Comments Connecting Mexican Immigrants and Crime" by Michele Ye Hee Lee. *Washington Post.* July 8, 2015.

54 Trump's response was "The wall just got 10 feet higher": "Donald Trump's Mexico Border Wall Will Be as High as 55 Feet, According to Donald Trump" by Philip Bump. *Washington Post.* February 26, 2016.

54 As time passed, however, Trump's promise began to shift: "A Fence, Steel Slats or 'Whatever You Want to Call It': A Detailed Timeline of Trump's Words About the Wall" by Kevin Quealy. *New York Times.* February 13, 2019. See also: "The Border Wall: What Has Trump Built So Far?" by Denise Lu. *New York Times.* February 12, 2019.

54 or even to stand in line at food banks in Washington, D.C.: "Food Banks Fill In for Paychecks as Government Shutdown Drags On" by Fenit Nirappil. *Washington Post.* January 19, 2019.

55 Speaking to Customs and Border Protection officers in Nogales, Arizona: "Attorney General Jeff Sessions Delivers Remarks Announcing the Department of Justice's Renewed Commitment to Criminal Immigration Enforcement." Remarks as Prepared for Delivery. Office of Public Affairs, Department of Justice. April 11, 2017.

57 These days, drugs like fentanyl and ecstasy flow into the U.S. from Canada: "Trump Is Freaking Out About the Wrong Bor-

der: Killer Fentanyl Is Coming from Canada" by Christopher Moraff. *Daily Beast.* April 9, 2018.

57 Canada has the most estimated visa overstays: "Homeland Security Produces First Estimate of Foreign Visitors to U.S. Who Overstay Deadline to Leave" by Jeffrey S. Passel and D'Vera Cohn. Pew Research Center. February 3, 2016.

59 Nowadays, though, Melilla is a different place: "Why Trying to Secure a 'Border' Is Futile" by Laila Lalami. *Los Angeles Times.* September 11, 2014.

62 these women, some of whom are in their fifties and sixties: "Facing (as) the Unexpected Access to Guarded Fields: Encounters with the Spanish Guardia Civil at a Border Crossing in Melilla" by Barak Kalir. *Border Criminologies Blog.* University of Oxford Faculty of Law. November 17, 2017.

62 In the makeshift camps where they live as they wait to cross: "Migrants Wait in Moroccan Forest for a Chance to Cross into Europe" by Leila Fadel. *Morning Edition.* NPR. April 21, 2016.

62 "If you come here every day": "The Heavy-Lifting 'Mule Women' of Melilla" by Linda Pressly. BBC World Service. October 30, 2013.

62 On his visit to China in 1972, Richard Nixon: Richard Nixon. "Exchange with Reporters at the Great Wall of China." February 24, 1972. The American Presidency Project. University of California, Santa Barbara.

62 Ronald Reagan gave a speech on East-West relations at the Brandenburg Gate: Ronald Reagan. "Remarks on East-West Relations at the Brandenburg Gate in West Berlin." June 12, 1987. The American Presidency Project. University of California, Santa Barbara.

63 in the three decades that followed, new walls have been built: "Le Monde se Referme: la Carte des Murs aux Frontières" by Camille Renard. *France Culture.* May 30, 2016.

63 Nowadays the West is constructing its own version of the Iron Curtain: "Our Walled World: How Walls Are Springing Up to Divide Us." *The Guardian.* November 19, 2013.

64 "We are human beings": "Checkpoint 300: Between Bethlehem and Jerusalem." Israel's TV Channel One. News Item. December 12, 2014.

65 they are sometimes referred to as "mujeres mulas": "Las 'Mujeres Mulas' que Cruzan Cada Día la Frontera entre España y Marruecos" *Público*. August 25, 2017. See also: "The Heavy-Lifting 'Mule Women' of Melilla" by Linda Pressly. BBC World Service. October 30, 2013.

65 On a visit to Calais in 2015: "Calais Crisis: Cameron Condemned for 'Dehumanising' Description of Migrants" by Jessica Elgot and Matthew Taylor. *The Guardian*. July 30, 2015.

65 one of his sons took to social media: "Donald Trump Jr. Compares Border Wall to Zoo Fences That Hold Animals in Instagram Post" by Jessica Durando. *USA Today*. January 9, 2019.

67 This power was tested in a landmark case known as *Martinez-Fuerte*: "The Praetorians: An Analysis of U.S. Border Patrol Checkpoints Following *Martinez-Fuerte*," by Jesus A. Osete. *Washington University Law Review* 803 (2016).

68 A few years ago, the residents of Arivaca: "Group Finds Racial Profiling at Amado Checkpoint—Latinos More Likely to Face Long Stops, ID Checks, Report Says." Yoohyun Jung and Perla Trevizo. *Arizona Daily Star*. October 20, 2014.

69 In May 2018, two American citizens: "A Border Agent Detained Two Americans Speaking Spanish. Now They Have Sued" by Liam Stack. *New York Times*. February 14, 2019.

69 that hundreds of Americans born in the Rio Grande valley: "U.S. Is Denying Passports to Americans Along the Border, Throwing Their Citizenship into Question" by Kevin Sieff. *Washington Post*. September 13, 2018.

ASSIMILATION

72 "The problem is," my seatmate said: "Blending In" by Laila Lalami. *New York Times Magazine*. August 5, 2017.

73 Newcomers represented an estimated 5 percent of population

growth: "The Contribution of Immigration to the Growth and Ethnic Diversity of the American Population" by Campbell Gibson. *Proceedings of the American Philosophical Society* 136, no. 2 (June 1992): 157–75.

73 "source of national wealth and strength": State of the Union Address by Abraham Lincoln. December 1863.

73 Harry Truman credited immigrants: "Text of Truman Message Calling for Admission of More European Refugees." *New York Times*. March 24, 1952.

74 In his *Notes on the State of Virginia*: *Notes on the State of Virginia* by Thomas Jefferson. Penguin Classics, 1998.

74 while "the red and the black assimilate": "The Chinese Within Our Gates." *New York Times*. July 20, 1890.

75 an event that led to another editorial in the *Times*: "The New Orleans Affair." *New York Times*. March 16, 1891.

75 By 1930, a Texas congressman named John C. Box: *Mongrels, Bastards, Orphans, and Vagabonds: Mexican Immigration and the Future of Race in America* by Gregory Rodriguez. Pantheon, 2007.

75 In November 1990, George H. W. Bush signed into law: "Statement on Signing the Immigration Act of 1990." November 29, 1990. The American Presidency Project. University of California, Santa Barbara.

76 The first time I saw Pat Buchanan on television: "1992 Pat Buchanan Presidential Campaign Announcement." C-SPAN clip. YouTube.

76 Donald Trump warned that "not everyone who seeks": "Trump Wants Immigrants to 'Share Our Values.' They Say Assimilation Is Much More Complex" by Hailey Branson-Potts. *Los Angeles Times*. April 11, 2017.

78 As mayor of Paris, Jacques Chirac famously lamented: "The New Inquisition" by Laila Lalami. *The Nation*. November 24, 2009.

79 founded by an army officer by the name of Richard Henry Pratt: *Official Report of the Nineteenth Annual Conference of Charities*

and Correction (1892), 46–59. Reprinted in Richard H. Pratt, "The Advantages of Mingling Indians with Whites," *Americanizing the American Indians: Writings by the "Friends of the Indian" 1880–1900.* Harvard University Press, 1973, 260–71.

79 The consequences of forced assimilation are still being felt centuries later: "American Indian Boarding Schools Haunt Many" by Charla Bear. *Morning Edition.* NPR. May 12, 2008.

79 Of the 300 distinct languages that were spoken in America: "Cultural Survival vs. Forced Assimilation: The Renewed War on Diversity" by Jon Reyhner. *Cultural Survival Quarterly Magazine.* June 2001. See also "What Was, and What Is: Native American Languages in the US" by Steph Koyfman. *Babbel Magazine.* October 4, 2017.

80 A special edition of the Bible: "Slave Bible from the 1800s Omitted Key Passages That Could Incite Rebellion" by Michel Martin. *All Things Considered.* NPR. December 9, 2018.

81 Malcolm declared flatly: "Malcolm X Debates Bayard Rustin (1962)" YouTube. See also: *Malcolm X: A Life of Reinvention* by Manning Marable. Viking, 2011. "Du Bois, Ghana and Cairo Jazz: The geo-politics of Malcolm X" by Hisham Aidi in *Routledge Handbook of Postcolonial Politics,* edited by Olivia U. Rutazibwa and Robbie Shilliam. Routledge, 2018.

82 These five million British citizens: "How many British immigrants are there in other countries?" by Oz Flanagan. American Statistical Association. 2014.

83 As many as one million Americans currently reside in Mexico: "America's Renegade Retirees" by Erin Siegal McIntyre. *U.S. News & World Report.* May 3, 2017.

87 English needed to retain its dominance: For some statistical data on this view, see "Nearly Half of White Republicans Say it Bothers Them to Hear People Speaking Foreign Languages" by Christopher Ingraham. *Washington Post.* May 8, 2019.

87 white working-class voters were 3.5 times more likely to support Donald Trump: "Beyond Economics: Fears of Cultural

Displacement Pushed the White Working Class to Trump" by Daniel Cox, Rachel Lienesch, and Robert P. Jones. Public Policy Research Institute. May 9, 2017.

89 "anti-Sharia measures": "Anti-Sharia Law Bills in the United States" by Swathi Shanmugasundaram. Southern Poverty Law Center. 2018.

89 In May 2015, more than two hundred armed activists: "Hundreds Gather in Arizona for Armed Anti-Muslim Protest" by Evan Wyloge. *Washington Post.* May 30, 2015.

90 Donald Trump once said that assimilation: "Trump Claims Assimilation Among American Muslims Is 'Close' to 'Nonexistent'" by Jose A. DelReal. *Washington Post.* June 15, 2016.

90 John Kelly, the former secretary of homeland security: "John Kelly on Trump, the Russia Investigation and Separating Immigrant Families" by John Burnett and Richard Gonzales. *Morning Edition.* NPR. May 10, 2018.

90 the journalist Tom Brokaw: "Tom Brokaw: 'Hispanics Should Work Harder at Assimilation'" by Rebecca Shapiro. *Huffington Post.* January 28, 2019.

90 surveys have consistently shown: "U.S. Muslims Concerned About Their Place in Society, but Continue to Believe in the American Dream." Pew Research Center. July 26, 2017.

91 while the rate of English proficiency: "English Proficiency Increasing Among Foreign-Born Hispanic Children." Hispanic Trends. Pew Research Center. May 11, 2015.

TRIBE

93 "But why"? my daughter asked: "Group Think" by Laila Lalami. *New York Times Magazine.* November 26, 2016.

95 "This is hilarious," the author told a bookstore audience: "Poking Fun at the 'Stuff White People Like.'" *Book Tour* segment by Neda Ulaby. NPR. September 2, 2008.

96 Ronald Reagan delivered outraged soliloquies: Reagan told the

"welfare queen" story repeatedly on the campaign trail in 1976. The specific quotes in this chapter are taken from a recording made available on *Slate Voice*. https://soundcloud.com/slate -articles/ronald-reagan-campaign-speech.

96 television ads about Willie Horton: "Willie Horton 1988 Attack Ad." YouTube.

96 Bill Clinton played a round of golf: The Clinton presidential campaign was chronicled in two great essays, "Eyes on the Prize" and "Clinton Agonistes," which appeared in *Political Fictions* by Joan Didion. Knopf, 2001.

96 allies of George W. Bush's presidential campaign: "The Trashing of John McCain" by Richard Gooding. *Vanity Fair*. November 2004. See also: "Read My Knuckles" by Eric Pooley. *Time*. February 28, 2000.

97 Immigration must be reformed, he said: "From Mexican Rapists to Bad Hombres, the Trump Campaign in Two Moments" by Janell Ross. *Washington Post*. October 20, 2016.

97 The big banks would not be held in check: "Donald Trump Deletes Tweet Showing Hillary Clinton and Star of David Shape" by Alan Rappeport. *New York Times.* July 2, 2016.

97 bad trade deals with China, which was "raping our country": "Trump: 'We Can't Continue to Allow China to Rape Our Country'" by Jeremy Diamond. CNN. May 2, 1016.

97 Football players who kneel in protest: "Donald Trump Blasts NFL Anthem Protesters: 'Get that Son of a Bitch off the Field'" by Bryan Armen Graham. *The Guardian*. September 23, 2017.

98 One is the term "white privilege": "White Privilege and Male Privilege: A Personal Account of Coming to See Correspondences Through Work in Women's Studies," by Peggy McIntosh. Working Paper No. 189. Wellesley College Center for Research on Women. 1988.

99 The second term is "white fragility": *White Fragility: Why It's So Hard for White People to Talk About Racism* by Robin DiAngelo. Beacon Press, 2018.

99 For example, a 1988 investigative report by Bill Dedman: "The

Color of Money" by Bill Dedman. *Atlanta Journal-Constitution*. 1988.

100 In a groundbreaking study in 2003: See "The Mark of a Criminal Record" by Devah Pager. *American Journal of Sociology* 108, no. 5 (2003): 937–75.

100 A recent study by the Economic Policy Institute: See "Black-White Wage Gaps Expand with Rising Wage Inequality" by Valerie Wilson and William M. Rodgers III. Economic Policy Institute. September 20, 2016. See also: "African Americans Are Paid Less Than Whites at Every Education Level" by Valerie Wilson. Economic Policy Institute. October 4, 2016.

104 In 1857, the Supreme Court ruled in *Dred Scott*: Material on the *Dred Scott v. Sandford* and *United States v. Wong Kim Ark* cases is available on Justia.com.

105 "total and complete shutdown of Muslims entering the United States": "Trump Calls for 'Total and Complete Shutdown of Muslims Entering the United States'" by Jenna Johnson. *Washington Post*. December 7, 2015.

106 a white lawyer went on a public rant: See "Lawyer Who Threatened to Call ICE About Spanish Speakers Is Now Target of Complaint" by Eli Rosenberg and Marwa Eltagouri. *Washington Post*. May 17, 2018.

106 a white student reported a black student: "A Black Yale Student Fell Asleep in Her Dorm's Common Room. A White Student Called Police" by Cleve R. Wootson, Jr. *Washington Post*. May 11, 2018.

106 a white mother called the police: "After Native American Bias Incident, College Says Those Against Diversity Can Go 'Elsewhere'" by Kristine Phillips. *Washington Post*. May 6, 2018.

106 waiting too long at a Starbucks in Philadelphia: "Men Arrested at Philadelphia Starbucks Speak Out; Police Commissioner Apologizes" by Amy Held. *The Two-Way*. NPR. April 19, 2018.

106 having a barbecue on Lake Merritt: "Video Shows Woman Calling Police over Barbecue at Lake Merritt" by Dianne de Guzman. *San Francisco Chronicle*. May 10, 2018.

106 playing a leisurely round of golf: "A Group of Black Women Say a Golf Course Called the Cops on Them for Playing Too Slow" by Tony Marco and Lauren DelValle. CNN. April 25, 2018.

106 checking out of an Airbnb in Rialto: "African-American Airbnb Customers Swarmed by Police Cars, Helicopter During Checkout" by Pritha Paul. *International Business Times.* May 8, 2018.

107 the Department of Education had handed out a checklist: "Education Department Withdraws 'Bomb Threat Checklist' That Used 'Ebonics' as an Identifier" by Valerie Strauss. *Washington Post.* November 20, 2017.

109 the argument that economic grievances: Exit poll results for the November 2016 election are available on CNN.com. See also: "How Groups Voted in 2016," a report from the Roper Center for Public Opinion Research at Cornell University. "White and Wealthy Voters Gave Victory to Donald Trump." *The Guardian.* November 9, 2016.

111 "a gentle loner": See "Robert Dear, Suspect in Colorado Killings, 'Preferred to Be Left Alone' " by Julie Turkewitz, Richard Fausset, Alan Blinder, and Benjamin Mueller. *New York Times.* November 28, 2015. The lead to the profile that included this language was rewritten after public outcry.

111 described Paddock as a "loner": "The Mystery of Stephen Paddock—Gambler, Real Estate Investor, Mass Killer" by Ruben Vives, Harriet Ryan, and Joseph Serna. *Los Angeles Times.* October 2, 2017.

111 the "slight" frame of Nikolas Cruz: "A Lost and Lonely Killer" by Brittany Wallman, Paula McMahon, Megan O'Matz, and Susannah Bryan. *Sun-Sentinel.* February 24, 2018.

112 But race is also an elastic fiction: *Whiteness of a Different Color: European Immigrants and the Alchemy of Race* by Matthew Frye Johnson. Harvard University Press, 1998.

114 Their legal status was initially decided in *Dow v. United States*: For a discussion of this case, see "Racing Religion" by Mustafa Bayoumi. *New Centennial Review* 6, no. 2 (Fall 2006): 267–93.

114 "Arabs as a class are not white": Material on *In Re Ahmed Hassan* can be found on Justia.com.

115 "vital interests [of the United States] as a world power": Material on *Ex Parte Mohriez* can be found on Justia.com.

115 they began to lobby: See "We Ain't White," in Hisham Aidi's *Rebel Music*. Pantheon, 2014.

CASTE

120 "freeloading at the expense of conscientious citizens": "Reagan Enters Gubernatorial Race in California: Speaking on TV, He Appeals for Support in Fight Against Rule by 'Big Brother'" by Peter Bart. *New York Times*. January 5, 1966.

120 growing by as many as 40,000 new recipients each month: "Reagan Ignored Pitfalls of Welfare." *Lodi News-Sentinel*. June 12, 2004.

120 he tightened eligibility rules for welfare: "California Legislature Approves Welfare Reform Bill After Compromise with Reagan." *New York Times*. August 12, 1971.

121 the state already spent $72 million a year: "Wilson's Political Fingerprints. Fingerprinting AFDC Recipients Will Be Costly and Won't Help, but It Works Well in the Governor's Campaign Sound Bites." *Fresno Bee*. April 21, 1994.

121 The new requirement cost another $17 million a year: "Gov. Brown Signs Bill Eliminating Fingerprinting Requirements for Food Stamp Recipients" by Steve Harmon. *Mercury News*. October 6, 2011.

121 blurred the lines between the welfare system and the criminal justice system: "The Criminalization of Poverty" by Kaaryn Gustafson. *Journal of Criminal Law and Criminology* 99, no. 3 (Summer 2009): 643–716.

123 The justification for the restriction: *The Right to Vote* by Alexander Keyssar. Basic Books, 2009.

125 There are fewer workers in unions: "Why Workers Won't Unite" by Kim Phillips Fein. *The Atlantic*. April 2015.

125–126 The representative from Texas's 10th Congressional District: Ballotpedia entry for Michael McCaul.

129 as James Baldwin put it: "Fifth Avenue, Uptown" by James Baldwin. *Esquire*. 1960.

131 According to the Census Bureau: "Income and Poverty in the United States: 2017" by Kayla Fontenot, Jessica Semega, and Melissa Kollar. U.S. Census Bureau. September 12, 2018. Report Number P60-263. See also: "Income and Poverty in the United States: 2017—Current Population Reports" by Jessica Semega, Kayla Fontenot, and Melissa Kollar. U.S. Census Bureau. September 2018. Report Number P60-263.

131 Women make, on average, 80 cents for every dollar a man makes: "What Is the Gender Pay Gap and Is It Real? The Complete Guide to How Women Are Paid Less Than Men and Why It Can't Be Explained Away" by Elise Gould, Jessica Schieder, and Kathleen Geier. Economic Policy Institute. October 20, 2016.

131 it excluded service workers and farm laborers: "The National Association for the Advancement of Colored People and New Deal Reform Legislation: A Dual Agenda" by Dona Cooper Hamilton. *Social Service Review* 68, no. 4 (1994): 488–502. See also: "The Racial Basis of Capitalism and the State, and the Impact of the New Deal on African Americans" by Steve Valocchi. *Social Problems* 41, no. 3 (August 1994): 347–62.

132 At its inception in 1935: "From Widow to 'Welfare Queen': Welfare and the Politics of Race" by Premilla Nadasen. *Black Women, Gender and Families* 1, no. 2 (Fall 2007): 52–77. See also: "The Criminalization of Poverty" by Kaaryn Gustafson. *Journal of Criminal Law and Criminology* 99, no. 3 (Summer 2009): 643–716.

133 programs benefiting the poor receive different support: "'Race Coding' and White Opposition to Welfare" by Martin Gilens. *American Political Science Review* 90, no. 3 (September 1996): 593–604.

133 In July 1992, when Bill Clinton accepted the Democratic nomi-

nation: "In Their Own Words: Transcript of Speech by Clinton Accepting Democratic Nomination." *New York Times.* July 17, 1992.

133 Twenty-five years later, standing on the steps of the Capitol: "Remarks of President Donald J. Trump, as Prepared for Delivery." Inaugural Address. January 20, 2017. White House website.

134 The British sociologist T. H. Marshall argued: *Citizenship and Social Class* by T. H. Marshall. Cambridge University Press. 1950.

135 just three Americans: "The 3 Richest Americans Hold More Wealth Than Bottom 50% of the Country, Study Finds" by Noah Kirsch. *Forbes.* November 9, 2017.

INHERITANCE

140 a prepared statement, which had been made available: "Christine Blasey Ford's Prepared Statement." *New York Times.* September 26, 2018.

141 "it was hard for me to breathe": "High-Stakes Duel of Tears and Fury Unfold in Senate" by Sheryl Gay Stolberg and Nicholas Fandos. *New York Times.* September 27, 2018.

141 she was confused about the identity of her attacker: "Updates from the Riveting Testimonies of Christine Blasey Ford and Brett Kavanaugh" by Charlie Savage. *New York Times.* September 27, 2018.

141 A week before the Senate hearing, Ed Whelan: "Conservative Activist Ed Whelan Apologizes for Insinuating a Kavanaugh Doppelgänger Assaulted Ford" by Jane Coaston. *Vox.* September 21, 2018.

143 "The oath of testimony": Shevu'ot 30.

143 "women should remain silent in the churches": Corinthians 14:34.

143 "if there are not two men [available]": Al-Baqarah 2:282.

146 my sister pressed into my hands a volume: *Beyond the Veil: Male-*

Female Dynamics in Modern Muslim Society by Fatima Mernissi. Schenkman Publishing. 1975. Reprinted by Indiana University Press. 1987. See also: *The Veil and the Male Elite: A Feminist Interpretation of Women's Rights in Islam* by Fatima Mernissi. Basic Books, 1991.

147 when she became the first woman: "Bouchra Bernoussi femme pilote de la RAM." Bladi.net. April 16, 2006.

150 I remember how the sociologist Soumaya Naamane Guessous: *Au-delà de toute pudeur: la sexualité féminine au Maroc* by Soumaya Naamane-Guessous. Editions Eddif, 1988.

152 when Brett Kavanaugh's turn came to testify: "Brett Kavanaugh's Opening Statement: Full Transcript." *New York Times.* September 27, 2019.

153 In fact, she had: "California Professor, Writer of Confidential Brett Kavanaugh Letter, Speaks Out About Her Allegation of Sexual Assault" by Emma Brown. *Washington Post.* September 16, 2018.

154 "My original intent was first and foremost to be a helpful citizen": "Christine Blasey Ford: 'My Fear Will Not Hold Me Back from Testifying" by Kate Sullivan and Manu Raju. CNN. September 24, 2018.

154 Over the course of two years: Nomination of Judge Clarence Thomas to Be Associate Justice of the Supreme Court of the United States. Hearings Before the Committee on the Judiciary. United States Senate 102nd Congress. Library of Congress.

Bibliography

Ahmed, Leila. *A Quiet Revolution: The Veil's Resurgence from the Middle East to America.* Yale University Press, 2011.

_____. *Women and Gender in Islam: Historical Roots to a Modern Debate.* Yale University Press, 1992.

Aidi, Hisham D. *Rebel Music: Race, Empire, and the New Muslim Youth Culture.* Pantheon, 2014.

Alexander, Michelle. *The New Jim Crow: Mass Incarceration in the Age of Colorblindness.* The New Press, 2010.

Anzaldúa, Gloria. *Borderlands / La Frontera: The New Mestiza.* Aunt Lute Books, 1987.

Balderrama, Francisco E., and Raymond Rodriguez. *Decade of Betrayal: Mexican Repatriation in the 1930s.* University of New Mexico Press, 1995.

Baldwin, James. *The Fire Next Time.* Dial Press, 1963.

_____. *No Name in the Street.* Dial Press, 1972.

_____. *Notes of a Native Son.* Beacon Press, 1955.

Coates, Ta-Nehisi. *Between the World and Me.* Spiegel & Grau, 2015.

Didion, Joan. *Political Fictions.* Knopf, 2001.

Fanon, Frantz. *The Wretched of the Earth.* Grove, 1963.

Galeano, Eduardo. *Genesis.* Quartet Books, 1985.

GhaneaBassiri, Kambiz. *A History of Islam in America: from the New World to the New World Order.* Cambridge University Press, 2010.

Hoig, Stan. *Beyond the Frontier: Exploring Indian Country.* University of Oklahoma Press, 1998.

Jefferson, Thomas. *Notes on the State of Virginia*. Penguin Classics, 1998.

Jones, Martha S. *Birthright Citizens: A History of Race and Rights in Antebellum America*. Cambridge University Press, 2018.

Keyssar, Alexander. *The Right to Vote*. Basic Books, 2009.

Lalami, Laila. "Blending In." *New York Times Magazine*. August 5, 2017.

_____. "Conditional Citizens." *The Nation*. October 10, 2016.

_____. "For or Against." *New York Times Magazine*. November 29, 2015.

_____. "Group Think." *New York Times Magazine*. November 26, 2016.

_____. "Love and Betrayal in America." *New Yorker* online. February 3, 2017.

_____. "The New Inquisition." *The Nation*. November 24, 2009.

_____. "Over the Edge." *New York Times Magazine*. April 29, 2017.

_____. "Walled Off." *The Nation*. June 3–10, 2019.

_____. "Why Trying to Secure a 'Border' Is Futile." *Los Angeles Times*. September 11, 2014.

Lepore, Jill. *This America: The Case for the Nation*. Liveright, 2019.

Lorde, Audre. *Sister Outsider*. Crossing Press, 2007.

Luiselli, Valeria. *Tell Me How It Ends: An Essay in 40 Questions*. Coffee House Press, 2017.

Majid, Anouar. *Islam and America: Building a Future Without Prejudice*. Rowman and Littlefield, 2012.

_____. *We Are All Moors: Ending Centuries of Crusades Against Muslims and Other Minorities*. University of Minnesota Press, 2009.

Marable, Manning. *Malcolm X: A Life of Reinvention*. Viking, 2011.

Margulies, Joseph. *What Changed When Everything Changed: 9/11 and the Making of National Identity*. Yale University Press, 2013.

Marshall, T. H. *Citizenship and Social Class*. Cambridge University Press, 1950.

Marzouki, Ahmed. *Tazmamart, Cellule 10*. Tarik Editions, 2000.

Mernissi, Fatima. *Beyond the Veil: Male-Female Dynamics in Modern Muslim Society*. Schenkman Publishing, 1975. Reprinted by Indiana University Press, 1987.

_____. *The Veil and the Male Elite: A Feminist Interpretation of Women's Rights in Islam*. Basic Books, 1991.

Morrison, Toni. *Playing in the Dark: Whiteness and the Literary Imagination*. Harvard University Press, 1992.

Naamane-Guessous, Soumaya. *Au-delà de toute pudeur: la sexualité féminine au Maroc*. Editions Eddif, 1988.

Nevins, Joseph. *Operation Gatekeeper: The Rise of the "Illegal Alien" and the Remaking of the U.S.-Mexico Boundary*. Routledge, 2001.

Nguyen, Viet Thanh, ed. *The Displaced: Refugee Writers on Refugee Lives*. Abrams, 2018.

Oufkir, Malika, and Michèle Fitoussi. *La Prisonnière*. Grasset, 1999.

Park, Thomas K., and Aomar Boum. *Historical Dictionary of Morocco*. 2nd ed. Scarecrow Press, 2006.

Rankine, Claudia. *Citizen: An American Lyric*. Graywolf Press, 2014.

Rodriguez, Gregory. *Mongrels, Bastards, Orphans, and Vagabonds: Mexican Immigration and the Future of Race in America*. Pantheon, 2007.

Said, Edward W. *Orientalism*. Pantheon Books, 1978.

_____. *Out of Place*. Knopf, 1999.

Serhane, Abdelhak. *Kabazal: Les Emmurés de Tazmamart. Mémoires de Salah et Aïda Hachad*. Tarik Editions, 2003.

Shaheen, Jack. *Reel Bad Arabs: How Hollywood Vilifies a People*. Olive Branch Press, 2014.

Shehadeh, Raja. *Where the Line Is Drawn: A Tale of Crossings, Friendships, and Fifty Years of Occupation in Irsael-Palestine*. The New Press, 2017.

Smarsh, Sarah. *Heartland: A Memoir of Working Hard and Being Broke in the Richest Country on Earth*. Scribner, 2018.

Smith, Stephen. *Oufkir: Un Destin Marocain*. Calmann-Lévy, 1999.

Twain, Mark. *Adventures of Huckleberry Finn*, 1885.

Wright, Lawrence. *The Looming Tower: Al Qaeda and the Road to 9/11*. Knopf, 2006.

X, Malcolm and Alex Haley. *The Autobiography of Malcolm X*. New York: Ballantine, 1992.

Acknowledgments

Portions of this book appeared, in earlier forms, in *The Nation, The Los Angeles Times, The New York Times Magazine,* and *The New Yorker* online. Many thanks to the editors who've solicited my work over the years. I am grateful to Santa Monica Arts for a travel fellowship; the Lannan Foundation for a residency in Marfa, Texas; the Simpson Literary Project for financial support at a crucial time; and the University of California at Riverside libraries for access to valuable resources. Thank you to my editor, Erroll McDonald, who offered judicious comments that improved the manuscript. Thank you to my agent, Ellen Levine, who has been a loyal advocate for many years. My publicists, Michiko Clark and Kimberly Burns, are the greatest champions a writer could have. Nicholas Thomson at Pantheon and Martha Wydysh at Trident Media always work hard on my behalf. Miriam Feuerle, Hannah Scott, Andrew Wetzel, and Kate Gannon-Sprinkel at Lyceum have supported my work in a myriad ways. I'm indebted to my dear friends Hisham Aidi, Brian Colker, Scott Martelle, Maaza Mengiste, and Viet Thanh Nguyen for their comments, questions, and encouragement. Thank you, as always, to Alexander Yera.

A Note About the Author

Laila Lalami was born in Rabat and educated in Morocco, Great Britain, and the United States. She is the author of four novels, including *The Moor's Account,* which won the American Book Award, the Arab-American Book Award, the Hurston/Wright Legacy Award and was a finalist for the Pulitzer Prize. Her most recent work, *The Other Americans,* was a finalist for the National Book Award. Her essays have appeared in the *Los Angeles Times,* the *Washington Post, The Nation, Harper's, The Guardian,* and the *New York Times.* She is the recipient of fellowships from the British Council, the Fulbright Program, and the Guggenheim Foundation, and is currently a professor of creative writing at the University of California at Riverside. She lives in Los Angeles.

A Note on the Type

This book was set in Granjon, a type named in compliment to Robert Granjon, a type cutter and printer active in Antwerp, Lyons, Rome, and Paris from 1523 to 1590. Granjon, the boldest and most original designer of his time, was one of the first to practice the trade of typefounder apart from that of printer.

Linotype Granjon was designed by George W. Jones, who based his drawings on a face used by Claude Garamond (ca. 1480–1561) in his beautiful French books. Granjon more closely resembles Garamond's own type than do any of the various modern faces that bear his name.

Typeset by Scribe, Philadelphia, Pennsylvania

Printed and bound by Berryville Graphics,
Berryville, Virginia

Designed by Betty Lew